Outside the Lines of

Gilded Age Baseball

Alcohol, Fitness, and Cheating in 1880s Baseball

Also by Rob Bauer

Nonfiction

Outside the Lines of Gilded Age Baseball: Gambling, Umpires, and Racism in 1880s Baseball

Outside the Lines of Gilded Age Baseball: The Origins of the 1890 Players League

Outside the Lines of Gilded Age Baseball: The Finances of 1880s Baseball

Fiction

My Australian Adventure

The World Traveler

The Buffalo Soldier

Darkness in Dixie

The Long Way Home

Outside the Lines of Gilded Age Baseball

Alcohol, Fitness, and Cheating in 1880s Baseball

Rob Bauer

For any inquiries regarding this book, please contact Rob at robbauerbooks@gmail.com.

For Mom

Thanks for everything.

Contents

Introduction   1

1. Abusing Alcohol   6

2. Limiting Alcohol Abuse   41

3. Beliefs About Player Fitness   72

4. Methods of Keeping Fit   90

5. Cheating and Dishonest Play   116

6. Violence on the Field   132

Epilogue   155

Notes on Statistics   159

Terminology of the 1880s   164

Bibliography   167

Index   169

About the Author   181

Acknowledgments   182

Introduction

Why write a book on the habits of players in 1880s baseball? This is, in fact, two questions posing as one. For starters, why write about baseball in the nineteenth century? It is, beyond doubt, the least studied era of the sport's history. Although baseball became a professional sport with an organized major league in 1871, we understand this period poorly and have understudied it severely compared to the rest of baseball's history. Names that any fan living in 1890 would have recognized instantly, such as John Ward, Dan Brouthers, John Clarkson, or Roger Connor, barely register today, even among many well-informed baseball observers. It is true that a few names have stood the test of time, but usually for reasons other than the quality of the person's play. We remember Cap Anson, for instance, for helping draw baseball's color line preventing African Americans from playing in the major leagues for several decades to come. Mike Kelly's name rings a bell with some because of his identification with novel methods of cheating and bending the rules. Many recognize Charlie Comiskey's name, but only because he later became the owner of the Chicago White Sox and has a ballpark named after him.

It is as if, for some reason, baseball fans and a few of its historians decided that baseball history really started in the year

1901. Even though a few reasons exist for this tendency, the reasons are more arbitrary than logical in most cases. The year is convenient, for one thing, because counting from 1901 takes in the entire twentieth century. That is also the year that the American League began play, challenging the National League's monopoly on major league baseball and giving us the two-league format major league baseball retains to the present. It is also true that most of the major changes to the rules of the game were in place by 1901, although a few exceptions exist. In addition, the schedule of 1901 was nearly the same length as that of today, as well, so any comparison of the performances between seasons include a roughly equal number of games.

On closer examination, however, we have many good reasons why choosing 1901 as the watershed year for baseball history is a poor choice. To begin with, the game on the field did not suddenly change in any recognizable way with the turn of the century. If we magically teleported back in time to the year 1885 and watched a baseball game, we would know exactly what we were watching and have no doubt it was baseball. True, the pitcher would be closer to home plate, and he would stand in a box instead of on a mound. The batter could request a high or low pitch from the pitcher. Not all the fielders wore gloves. Only one umpire would be on the field, and there might not be a fence enclosing the field of play. All these things would look a little strange to us, but still, once play began, it would be baseball, no doubt about it.

In fact, the game as played in 1890 resembled the game of 1910 a lot more than the game of 1910 resembled the game of 1930. Both 1890 and 1910 featured ballparks with large dimensions where home runs were difficult to come by. In 1910, wood remained the construction material of choice for many major league ballparks, limiting the number of fans who might attend the game. The concrete-and-steel behemoths we expect to see today were in place by the 1930s, however. In the 1930s, although the ballpark itself was much larger and seated tens of thousands of fans, the field of play was usually smaller. This difference in the dimensions of the field meant that having athletic, speedy players on defense was very important in 1890 or 1910, whereas by 1930 it was possible to win games with a lineup of strapping power hitters who rarely took chances on the base paths and had less ground to patrol while in the field. Even a cursory glance at stolen base totals by season confirms this, although changes made to the ball also had something to do with baseball's shift toward the home run as an important strategy. In any case, the 1930s strategy of waiting for power hitters to wallop the ball over the fence was a new way to play baseball and one that would be no more likely to succeed in 1910 than it was in 1890.

For the players on the field, the game at the end of the nineteenth century was little different from the game of the early twentieth century, either. It is not as though they woke up on January 1, 1901, and suddenly realized that a new era had dawned for major league baseball. The best players of 1901 were the same men who had been the best players in 1900. There were more players in major league baseball thanks to the emergence of the American League, but it was not as though success in baseball suddenly demanded an entirely new set of skills. The incomparable Honus Wagner led the National League in Wins Above Replacement (WAR) among position players in 1900. He also led National League position players in WAR for eight straight years from 1902 to 1909, as well as in 1911 and 1912, even though he was thirty-eight years old by 1912, so clearly, it was not hard to adapt to playing in a new century.

Whatever the reasons, even if those reasons are not very strong ones, many baseball observers either ignore or place less weight on the events of the nineteenth century. In a sense, this book and its three companions are my modest attempt to balance things up a little bit and try to give the nineteenth-century game more of the attention it deserves. Not only that, but everything I have found in my research indicates that the game of the 1880s would be enjoyable to play and watch. Other than the chance of an opponent punching you or having a flying beer glass strike you, perhaps. The game of the late-nineteenth century was a game of motion and action. Today's version of baseball, where games lasting three hours or more are the norm and a never-ending series of pitching changes break up the action in the late innings and numb the fans, would be anathema to spectators in the Gilded Age. They would not stand for it. In the 1880s, a typical game took about half the time it takes to play nine innings today, and whenever team owners considered changing the rules of the game, their goal was producing more action on the field to please the spectators. Sounds like fun.

Besides attempting to bring more attention to the early years of professional baseball, I've also investigated the question of player habits and behavior. Again, this is an area of the game's history largely unknown and rarely discussed in most books. Many baseball fans know that various star players had certain habits or characteristics. Babe Ruth and Mickey Mantle liked to drink and have a good time after games, for instance. This does not tell us much, however, about whether drinking by players was widespread in their eras, or limited to just a few charismatic individuals. Nor do we know what precautions teams took, if any, to limit drinking by players or if spectators even cared how much players might drink.

To take another example, Philadelphia and Boston first baseman Jimmie Foxx was among the strongest men ever to play baseball, at least before the days of modern weightlifting and scientific training. Did his success trigger a movement toward finding big, strong men to anchor the middle of a team's lineup, or was he considered so exceptional that it was pointless to even try to emulate him? Did other players of the 1930s adopt any kind of training regimen to be more like Foxx or do things outside of the regular season to be in peak physical condition? Again, we do not know very much about these questions, all things considered. It is a part of baseball history that deserves more attention, and my series of books on 1880s baseball tries to address some of these important questions about the behavior of players as a group and what that meant for the way people played baseball and its popularity with the public.

Introduction

It is also a good idea to learn more about the habits and off-field lives of professional baseball players because this knowledge helps cut through the fog of nostalgia that surrounds the game and gives us a more realistic picture of what it was like to be a ballplayer in the Gilded Age. It seems to me that while the game itself probably was a lot of fun to play, many of the players were not especially likable people. Center fielder Curt Welch, for instance, had a reputation as a respectable hitter and marvelous defensive outfielder, but he was also a drunkard and a thug, if we can believe what contemporaries said and wrote about him. Other players, like New York first baseman Roger Connor, would have a reputation as a gentleman in any era, while men like John Ward possessed quick and active minds. Most, however, were men of the time, which meant hardscrabble, working-class people. Alcoholism was rampant. Players drank often and as a result also fought and argued often. Baseball might have begun as a recreational game mostly played by athletic clubs featuring well-heeled gentlemen, but that part of its history was long gone by the 1880s. The men of the Gilded Age played for keeps, and no rule was so sacred that players would not break it if the umpire turned his back for a moment. Any thoughts the reader might entertain about players playing simply for the love of the game or the thrill of a championship are out of place in 1880s baseball. A few men did play for the enjoyment of the game, undoubtedly, but for most of them baseball was their profession and, like any professional, they expected professional pay and respect.

This, then, is the story of how players behaved in 1880s baseball. It is, by turns, funny, depressing, informative, and sometimes just weird. In other words, a lot like regular peoples' lives, but set against the backdrop of professional sports. I hope you enjoy the journey.

Chapter 1

Abusing Alcohol

In Gilded Age baseball one behavior of ballplayers threatened the game more than any other: the abuse of alcohol. Besides trying to keep salaries down, nothing vexed baseball's owners more than the issue of player drinking. Team captains and managers constantly fretted over whether a key player would arrive at the grounds to play ball in a sober condition. Possibly the only thing that ruined more productive careers than alcohol was a dreaded arm injury. Often, when sportswriters reminisced about this or that player from the past, they had to preface their remarks with some comment reflecting the greatness that had been within a player's reach, had that man only avoided the lure of the bottle.

Therefore, while it is interesting, and at times tragic, to examine the drinking escapades of certain players in detail, it is important to keep in mind that these men were not isolated problems. They were simply the most notable manifestations of an exceptionally widespread problem bedeviling baseball in the 1880s. Even a casual perusal of the sporting papers of the late 1880s reveals that issues of sobriety and player fitness were enormously important. Almost every single team featured men who drank to excess on occasion, if not oftener. Even for those men who abstained from liquor during the playing season, the off-season might be a different story altogether. Hard as it might be to believe in the modern era where observers tend to view baseball through a statistical lens, in the 1880s a player's perceived sobriety level was usually the second most important consideration teams had when deciding whether to sign a new man, trailing only the talent of the player. In addition to teams making personnel decisions based on the drinking habits of the men involved, the news articles discussing the trades and releases of players frequently mentioned drinking habits as part of the justification for the decision to let a man go.

We should note that, for the most part, baseball players were no different from the society around them when it came to drinking habits. People, men especially, drank frequently in the 1880s. Alcohol was central to working-class culture—part of the passage to manhood—and many ballplayers and fans came out of this culture. After a ten-, twelve-, or even fourteen-hour shift mining coal, making steel, or milling timber, workers were tired. Rather than go home and collapse, however, they often visited the neighborhood saloon to enjoy time with their fellows and blow off steam. Many working-class people had little to do at home other than spend time with the family and read a newspaper if the person was literate, and many were not. Home, in many cases, was a cramped, poorly ventilated, and in the summer, blisteringly-hot apartment, anyway. Television and radio did not exist in the 1880s, either. Most people preferred to spend their free time out in public or in a drinking establishment.

Saloons and bars provided more than just drinks, too. Many also performed the functions of post offices and job placement agencies, especially in the larger ethnic neighborhoods of America's cities. An immigrant from northern Germany who only spoke German might go to the neighborhood saloon so he could meet others who spoke German. Immigrants who had been in the country for a few years and understood how things worked might help a newcomer find employment or housing. The newcomer could also hear songs in his native language, read a newspaper printed in German, and so forth. Even for those who had been in America for several generations, saloons served some of these same functions. In cities and larger towns, they were a central feature of the landscape.

A look at who some of the men with weaknesses for alcohol were, and what stories their drinking escapades inspired, gives a good idea of how important alcohol was to the game in the 1880s. A classic example comes from Cincinnati in 1886. That year, the Red Stockings were members of the American Association, and what happened to them is a good example of how the temptation to sign heavy drinkers might drag down a team. In 1885 the Red Stockings had been a strong team, posting a 63-49 record. That record put them in second place in the American Association, but the champion St. Louis Browns were a very strong team, and the Red Stockings ended the campaign sixteen games back. So, when the off-season arrived, Cincinnati's management looked for some new blood to strengthen its nine and put the team over the top in 1886.

In November, the team thought it had found its men, outfielder Fred Lewis and pitcher Billy Taylor, but many observers lacked conviction that the team had done rightly. In its description of the transaction, *The Sporting Life*'s correspondent reported with disgust that the Red Stockings had signed two players known for their tendency to imbibe freely: "These are two disturbers who were cleaned out from the Association last year, and should be kept out forever. Both are good players when they are in condition, but it is folly to expect them to keep straight. The National Agreement should make a rule for the permanent blacklisting of such men, so that clubs will not be tempted to take them up."[1] In justifying this view, sportswriter O. P. Caylor recalled the 1884 incident in which Lewis, playing on the St. Louis Browns at the time, so enraged Browns owner Chris Von der Ahe with his drinking habits that Von der Ahe suspended him indefinitely for his lushing. Furious, Lewis "grabbed a bat and started to hunt up Chris." The owner beat the player to the safety of the clubhouse by a nose, at which point he decided Lewis' suspension unjustified, after all.[2] After that event, whenever Von der Ahe wanted to discuss player drinking, he tended to describe it as "conduct . . . of the Fred Lewis order."[3]

Aware of his shaky reputation, Lewis hoped to dispel, or at least allay, the fears of his doubters. He got off to a good start, too. Lewis, who "has written a letter to the Cincinnati Club management in which he asserts that he will play ball for all he is worth next season"[4] according to *The Sporting Life*, had a fine season for the Red Stockings in 1886, ranking among the league's leading hitters for part of the season and sporting a .318/.365/.417 batting line in 77 games for a robust OPS+ of 142. It was his last season in the majors, however, and coming at age twenty-seven, when most players reach their prime, his bad habits were to blame for his early departure.[5]

This was because, sadly, Lewis did not complete the season and capitalize on his strong start. A broken ankle shelved him in August, which was a true shame for both him and the Red Stockings because Lewis was second in the American Association in batting average at the time.[6] Following the layoff, *The Sporting News* reported that Lewis's old habits had returned: "Lewis, the center fielder, who last year was one of the heaviest batters of the League, has been behaving very badly. He is drunk a great deal of the time, and is utterly worthless because of his convivial habits. He will undoubtedly be sent to find another engagement."[7] The same paper blamed his teammates: "Many ballplayers firmly believe Fred Lewis would have stayed sober this season had the Cincinnati Club played better ball. Fred, it is claimed, became discouraged at the club's continued hard luck, and utter indifference with which some of the team played while away from home."[8]

This failure led to the end of Lewis' major league career. The 1887 season found Lewis playing for Rochester in the International

League. He made the news late in the season for, yes, drinking, when the Flour City club docked him fifty dollars after an appearance in police court.[9] It was his only season in Rochester, according to *The Sporting News*, because "the disgraceful antics of some of the players so disgusted the patrons and management that not a single player was reserved for next season. They were all released."[10] *The Sporting Life* reported that things did not improve for Lewis in 1888, either. In March, he spent ten days in a Utica, New York, jail after assaulting an alderman: "The latter is a saloon-keeper, and Lewis entered the saloon and struck the official for going back on one of his friends."[11]

Lewis' demise was a shame for himself and for baseball because, when he was not drinking, some of the sporting papers sang his praises: "Fred Lewis . . . is probably the finest specimen of an athlete in the baseball profession; without a particle of superfluous flesh or fat, he will weigh nearly two hundred pounds. . . . He is one of the hardest workers and one of the most quiet men on the team."[12] Furthermore, in training sessions before the season, Lewis impressed observers "by the ease and grace with which he handled the 100-pound weights. Fred says he will play the game of his life and his admirers know the meaning of that."[13] When his effort at reform showed promise in the early weeks of the 1886 season, O. P. Caylor described the result: "Fred Lewis has made this city his friend. He has begun to do what he promised he would—play the best ball of his life. He is a great favorite with the patrons of the club, with the club and with the team."[14]

Although, ultimately, Fred Lewis could not shake his old habits, he at least put up a decent front for most of 1886. Not so with Billy Taylor. When Cincinnati decided not to sign him, after all, he moved on to Baltimore to frustrate the fans and management there. He showed up in good form, but that was the best anyone could say about his time in the Monumental City. *The Sporting Life* reported how "Billy Taylor looks exceedingly well and appears to be in good condition. . . . He showed remarkable speed. Barnie, he says, will never regret engaging him."[15] Once the championship season began, however, it was a different story. Taylor posted a poor ERA+ of just 60. Manager Billy Barnie of Baltimore tried to cover his bases with Taylor via an "ironclad contract" that allowed Barnie to withhold some of Taylor's salary until the end of the month as "security for his good behavior."[16] Barnie should have required greater security because Taylor's behavior was not very good. He released Taylor after just eight games started, and by August Taylor was set to join his third team for the season, Milwaukee, following his release from Memphis of the Southern League.[17] Taylor's tenure in Memphis impressed no one, and the quantity of alcohol he imbibed rose to the point where he brought a gallon of brew to a game against Nashville.[18] Before the curtain dropped on 1886, papers reported he was at Mt. Carmel, Pennsylvania, and actually doing well because he had managed to lay off the fire water for a time.[19] After the 1886 season, however, Taylor's career took a similar trajectory as Lewis's, and Taylor pitched just one more game in major league baseball.

Taylor tried his best to convince someone in major league baseball to employ him in 1887, but by that time, he had tarnished his reputation so badly that no one believed his protestations of sobriety. He went on an off-season exhibition tour in the Spanish colony of Cuba over the winter, and wrote to a St. Louis sportswriter claiming just one drink had "passed his collar button" since arriving on the island. The writer replied, "The only way I can get around this story is that Bill either takes 'double' drinks or he doesn't wear such a thing as a collar button."[20] Despite the well-earned sarcasm, it appears Taylor was not lying. *The Sporting Life* mentioned that "President Morrow, of the Southern League, saw him in Cuba recently, and says that he has fallen off so much that he hardly knew him. He actually refused to take a drink when the handsome 'Pooh-Bah' of the Southern League offered to 'set 'em up.' Simmons, Scott and all the players who were in Cuba confirm this."[21] Sources also reported his abstention from spirits had helped him drop fifty pounds.[22] This led another writer to comment, "Billy Taylor is the metaphorical ground hog of base ball. He comes out of his hole about this time in the season and remarks that he has sworn off, sees the shadow of past transgressions, and then crawls back again to await the sunshine of managerial touching trust and child-like faith."[23]

Nonetheless, Taylor finally ran out of serious chances. He signed a deal with Charleston in the Southern League to start the 1887 season, and the writer describing the transaction showed his share of child-like faith in "Gay and Festive William": "He has by constant exercise reduced himself considerably and is in the pink of condition. . . . There has been considerable newspaper talk about Billy's lushing, etc., but when the time comes to play ball he will not be found wanting."[24] Taylor's performance in the Birthplace of Secession was found wanting, however, and by 1888 Taylor was back north of the Mason-Dixon Line in Scranton, Pennsylvania. It is unknown whether drink had anything to do with his behavior in one strange episode, but he was an accomplice when teammate Sam Crane eloped with a married woman in Scranton and carried off $1,400 of the married couple's money at the same time.[25] Nor was this the only time that Taylor mixed women and baseball. Once, he was the volunteer umpire for a game featuring two touring teams of women. After the game, he hopped on the omnibus with some of the women, and in the drunken cavorting that followed, married one of them.[26]

The last we hear of Taylor in baseball is when he and another player engaged to play for a team in Hot Springs, Arkansas, in 1889. Feeling good about their chances with a former professional pitcher on their side, Hot Springs fans bet heavily on their nine with Taylor in the points, but instead of helping the team to victory over Pine Bluff, he sold out to Pine Bluff for $50 and skipped town. This so incensed the good people of Hot Springs that they hired detectives to run Taylor to ground: "Detectives are looking for these people, and if they are caught it will go hard with them."[27] Sadly, we do not hear if the detectives succeeded in corralling Taylor, but clearly, his shady conduct marred his own promising career and hampered the efforts of his teammates over and over. It seems fair to say baseball was well rid of him.

Even if not all players drank to the extent of Taylor and Lewis, the problem was a general one, and fans and sportswriters knew it just as well as team officials did. The fact that a writer for *The Sporting Life* could provide readers with a report card on drinking among the various teams in 1885 shows that people around the game freely discussed the relationship between players and C_2H_5OH. "On the general average the teams of the Association were pretty temperate last year as to drinking. The Metropolitans and our own Athletics were about the worst," he wrote. Meanwhile, in Cincinnati, the "lushing tendencies which are growing upon the team" threatened to sabotage a promising run at the next league championship.[28]

Along the same lines, early in the 1889 season, the paper's Columbus correspondent gave a general indictment of the entire American Association: "I am told that the Columbus team is not alone in endeavoring to combine ball playing and lushing, and seeking to discover a winning combination in it, but that the Athletics are following the same tactics they used last year, and that even Kansas City and Louisville have players that are crooking the elbow oftener than the good results of base ball require." While the writer admitted he had no authority to influence team policy, for the good of the game, he implored his hometown team to do better, writing, "I am going to engage my pencil, while it lasts, in calling down the members of the Columbus team in their damphool efforts to sink the pastime of base ball into oblivion in this town plot, and use all my efforts to save the Columbus directors from a heavy financial loss that certain lushing ball players would in a cold-blooded, heartless manner seek to impose upon them."[29]

Part of the reason this writer knew so much about the behavior of players on other teams was that other papers reported the drinking habits of players to the public freely. When the Columbus nine played Kansas City, one paper wrote, "It is a wonder that Kansas City plays as well as it does, for it is no secret that several of the boys are lushing hard. A number of both Columbus and Kansas City players saw the sights last (Monday) night, and to those who were on the game was better than was expected."[30] The next week, Cincinnati fined catcher Billy Earle fifty dollars for arriving late because "It is not known whether he had been indulging in the ardent, but such is the supposition, as he was out the night previous later than usual, and the next morning he looked very blue."[31]

Signing men like Taylor or Lewis was risky, but teams often did so knowing that if the player could not control his drinking, it was easy to let a drinking man go at the end of the season. What happened, however, when the lushing players were the best players on the team? What did a team do with men who were too valuable to let go because even if drinking hurt their performance, their talent made them an asset anyway? The perfect case study of a person who fit this description was Mike Kelly, a superstar player for Chicago and Boston in the National League. He was, probably, the most popular player in 1880s baseball, and among the most talented. The stories concerning Kelly's drinking exploits were legion; describing all of them here would almost take its own chapter. He was the quintessential working-class boy who made good in baseball. Working-class spectators adored Kelly because he was one of them and he did not change after achieving baseball stardom. He was fun, talented, generous, and charismatic, all of which helped make him the biggest drawing card in baseball. Kelly also, however, had a weakness for alcohol and could be headstrong. According to some, he also tended to get depressed when his team was not winning.

There was an incident featuring Kelly in 1887 that showed how problematic his combination of traits might be when put in the wrong situation. That year the New York Giants, with a few other players in tow, including Kelly, visited New Orleans for some exhibition games in late October and early November. While most of the club, including such notable players as shortstop John Ward and pitcher Tim Keefe, walked the straight line during their stay in the Crescent City, not all their teammates maintained an honorable record in this regard. On Monday, three players, Kelly, third baseman Jerry Denny, and catcher Buck Ewing, arrived at the grounds in carriages accompanied by several drunken inhabitants of the city. After these inebriated cranks called out a continual stream of obscenities, New Orleans' Secretary Kaufmann summoned the police to remove the boors. In the words of New York's Keefe, "Our last game was well attended by a lot of Basin Street hoodlums, and from the time the game started until its close it was a constant stream of profanity that came from their quarters and intended for the New York players."[32] When the authorities arrived to remove the offenders, Kelly entered the stands and tried to prevent their arrest, and then, when the next inning began and New York was supposed to take the field, remained in the stands drinking beer rather than take his position. John Ward, mortified, sent his new wife, the noted actress Helen Dauvray Ward, back to the team hotel in a carriage. The officials of the New Orleans club were equally shocked, to the extent they informed Ward and the Giants that there would be no more exhibition games until Ward obtained an ironclad promise from all his men to play the games in a sober condition.[33]

All of Kelly's worst traits came together in another incident in July of 1888, when Boston dropped a couple games to the Philadelphia Quakers and Kelly decided to hit the town and "drowned his sorrows in something stronger than soda water." He did not return to the team hotel that evening and straggled in for the next game with the Quakers without his uniform. Kelly's actions forced Boston captain and manager John Morrill to give him a public reprimand, then borrow an extra uniform from Quakers manager Harry Wright for the game that day.[34]

True to his nature, an embarrassed Kelly decided to take extreme steps following this disgraceful incident. Even after Kelly's public reprimand, John Morrill despaired of ever getting Kelly to shape up.

One reporter wrote, "Manager Morrill has not fined him, but he frankly confesses he can do nothing with Kelly, who is so headstrong and willful, and has an idea he can do as he pleases. In fact, he has been doing as he pleased, and this is the reason of the trouble." As a result, Kelly became so remorseful that he decided to swear off booze: "Kelly asserts that he is done with drinking, and means to play ball from here out." The odds of Kelly keeping his pledge were long, but this brought a bit of peace to the Beantown nine for the time being.[35] Kelly also hinted, however, that strained relations with Boston were at the heart of his troubles because he also said, "There are two things that I am certain of. I intend to take the pledge and not drink a drop of liquor for a year. I have an offer to go into business next year and I will accept. I have no desire to play under this management any longer."[36]

Kelly's story is the same conundrum confronting the American Association's Louisville franchise and its tragicomic relationship with star players Tom Ramsey and Pete Browning. Ramsey was an ace pitcher with an ability to rack up strikeouts that was second to none in the 1880s. His career lasted just five full seasons, but he led the American Association in strikeouts per nine innings for two of those seasons, and retired 499 men on strikes in 1886. Browning was the team's star hitter, primarily playing the outfield over the course of a thirteen-year career. He led the league in batting three times, with a high of .402 in 1887, and his .341 lifetime batting average is among the highest of any player not in baseball's Hall of Fame.

Stories abound of Browning's antics, foibles, and strange decisions. Ever the character, before he became a major league player with Louisville, Browning played for a semi-professional team in the Falls City. One season, his club did not pay him in cash, but with a contract that promised him all the ice cream and cake he wanted to eat during the playing season. This cost his club something on the order of thirty dollars per month.[37] Although he allowed drinking to tarnish his play and had more than his share of quirks, he certainly had some redeeming qualities as well. One of

Browning's nicknames was "The Gladiator" because some perceived him as having a combative personality, but people also knew him as "The Louisville Slugger" because he was the first to contract with the company Hillerich and Bradsby to make the bats still known by that name today. He also saved a young Louisville boy from death in 1884. A team of horses pulling a streetcar was bearing down on the lad when Browning ducked in and pulled the youth to safety.[38]

The incredible thing about Browning was that, no matter how much alcohol he might drink and how much his defense might suffer, his hitting remained impeccable. His batting line for 1886 was .340/.389/.441, for an OPS+ of 155, and the next season he was far better, slashing .402/.464/.547 for an OPS+ of 177 even though he reported for the 1887 season in poor condition to begin with. As one writer opined, "This man's recuperative powers are wonderful. They must be fully equal to those of John L. Sullivan. Other base ball players have dissipated as much in a given time as Pete, but I know of no one who has kept it up as steadily for eight regular base ball years and can yet play a good game. And he is still an attraction wherever the club goes."[39] All this even though one day he came to the Louisville team meal at the Lindell Hotel in St. Louis drunk to the point that, when the waiter asked him what he wanted to eat, Browning declared he was not very hungry and would just have beaver eggs. When the uncomprehending waiter informed him the hotel did not offer beaver eggs, Browning took the menu to point out what he wanted. His finger eventually landed on the word beverages.[40]

We pick up their saga in 1886, when Browning was twenty-five years old and well-established as a star performer, but Ramsey was only twenty-one and just entering his first full season in major league baseball. Louisville appeared to be in good shape going into the 1886 season. The team had finished sixth place the year before at 53-59, but the emergence of Ramsey (he ended up starting 67 games in 1886) to team with star pitcher Guy Hecker gave them hope for the '86 campaign. However, with Louisville, there always was something wrong, always a catch, and one of their sportswriters pinpointed the problem: "The members of the club are all in splendid condition. . . . There are only two players of the club—Ramsey and Browning—who are addicted to the habit of strong drink, but Manager Hart is confident that they will be conspicuous during the coming season for steady behavior and quiet demeanor."[41] Manager Jim Hart might have had second thoughts when, seeing Ramsey report for the team's southern trip of exhibition games in March, "Ramsey came in at the last moment. He did not look in very good condition for playing, showing signs of dissipation."[42]

Off and on, the drinking issues persisted as the season stretched into July and August. During Louisville's late July road trip to the East Coast one of the writers covering the team stated, "President Phelps accompanied the boys on this trip. Result no lushing." Pete Browning was absent from the club by this time, however, recuperating from an eye injury. The same writer wrote of Browning, "It is a hard matter for Pete Browning to drink water at the Springs. He is not accustomed to it. He had the picture of a distillery hung in his room. It seemed to afford him much pleasure."[43] In Browning's defense, however, he suffered from acute mastoiditis, which caused him chronic pain and hearing loss, and this was probably part of his effort to deal with the pain, but still, it did not do much for the team's morale or performance.[44]

The personal attention of Phelps seemed to have helped Ramsey toe the line. For a time, at least. In mid-August one observer wrote, "Ramsey is pitching great ball and is taking the best care of himself. In consequence he has hundreds of friends now where he had one in the spring."[45] Ramsey could not keep it up, sadly. By late September, with the team's chances of catching the St. Louis Browns for first place fading like a rain puddle in the desert sun, "Ramsey from continual carousing and late hours has completely broken down and had to be sent to his home in Indianapolis. He is done playing for the remainder of the season."[46] Even though

Ramsey did pitch a few more games after this incident, the team's fortunes did not improve, and Louisville's fans ended 1886 wondering what might have been, especially when, about the same time that Ramsey's unsavory habits returned, Browning, too, allowed liquor to tarnish his play: "Browning has let down again in left field. Too much dissipation is said to be the cause. . . . He has gotten the idea that he can do very near as he pleases. There is no doubt as to his ability to play good ball when he wants to."[47]

In baseball, each new season is always a time of hope, but for Louisville's cranks, Ramsey and Browning called their hopes into question early in the 1887 season. Ramsey was the first man on the team fined by new manager John Kelly for his lack of commitment to his work. After some early season games in which his "spiritless and sulky playing was manifest to everybody,"[48] Ramsey stayed out boozing past 3:00 a.m. on a night before he was to pitch. Kelly put his foot down with authority: "Today you've been behaving yourself like a monkey and you've got to pay for it. You are fined the limit— fifty dollars—and every time you do this sort of thing again you'll get another fifty." At least Ramsey admitted the error of his ways, and allowed that Kelly had been right to fine him.[49]

Browning did not even pretend he planned to go easy on the liquor in 1887; rather, he made no secret of his fondness for strong drink. Before the season began, a writer asked him for his thoughts on the club's new manager, John Kelly. Browning replied, "He is a good one; but you can bet he won't bulldoze me. I am bound to have my allowance of rum, Kelly or no Kelly. Jim Hart tried to stop me from taking an occasional drink, but I learned him a thing or two." According to Browning, however, Kelly knew how to use demon rum as a motivating tool as well: "Kelly has promised each of us boys a new suit of clothes and a five-gallon keg of the best whiskey in Kentucky if we win the championship next season, so I would advise the rest of the clubs to look out for Louisville."[50] As much as Browning enjoyed tippling, however, there was probably no truth to the rumor that when he finally signed his contract for 1887, it was because saloon owners in Louisville forced him to, so he could pay off his tabs run up over the winter. He also knew better than to hit the bottle with sportswriters; he once told a story about excusing himself from a drink with one who had written negative stories about his lushing several times previously, going so far as to claim he was going to walk the straight path in 1887.[51]

Predictably, Kelly had to finesse the drinking issue with his two star players as the season progressed. Both men painted the town on drinking sprees in late August and early September, for which Kelly fined Browning fifty dollars and suspended Ramsey indefinitely without pay. Ramsey's arm was in bad shape by that time anyway, so the team did not really miss him, but Browning immediately caught fire with the ash after bracing up, smacking nineteen hits in his next five games. Because both men appeared remorseful, however, they quickly returned to Kelly's good graces. Nineteen hits in five games probably helped Browning, too.[52] By early October, however, he was in disgrace once again. During the season's closing week, the Colonels were battling their hated rivals from Cincinnati when Browning failed to turn up for the first game of the series. Badly intoxicated and unable to reach the train station in time, he'd missed the train from St. Louis altogether. Playing the next day, but still hung over badly, he managed to strike a double, but while taking his lead from second base, Cincinnati tagged him out when he fell asleep on the field. No wonder that, when John Kelly set off to scour the country for new talent in the 1887-1888 off-season, he said, "I will take only men of the very best class. I want them sober and reliable, so that I can always depend on them, and I won't have any others."[53]

Ramsey's experience in 1887 is also a good example of how, once earned, a bad reputation can be difficult to shed. While fully admitting to his fondness for drink, he claimed it had not ruined his performance on the field or hurt the Colonels in any significant way. Following the 1887 season, when Louisville again slumped late in the year, including four straight losses to the last place Cleveland club, and fell to fourth place in the standings, people blamed his drinking. Ramsey had had enough of the criticism: "I admit that I have been a little wrong once or twice, but I have always done my best when I was pitching. I want the club to succeed, and I help it as much as I can. . . . I have pitched in more games and won more than all the other pitchers in the nine put together, and all I ask is fair and considerate treatment from the people." (He was almost correct—he won 37 games that year out of 76 wins for the whole team.) A Louisville sportswriter agreed, stating that while he knew Ramsey imbibed at times, "There are men in this and other clubs who drink more. He is not so shrewd about it as they are, and gets caught oftener." The writer followed up this lukewarm defense of the talented pitcher by writing, "Ramsey is honest. Manager Kelly can depend on him. When the pitcher says that he will do a certain thing Manager Kelly can believe him, and considers his word sufficient."[54]

The reader can imagine the baseball world's shock, therefore, when news arrived in April of 1888 that the Louisville club, every single player, took the blue-ribbon pledge of abstinence just prior to the season. Seemingly, it took an act of God to achieve this in 1880s baseball, and that is exactly what the Colonels' management produced, in the person of noted temperance evangelist Francis Murphy. He gave the players a lengthy harangue, and "the players seemed considerably affected by his remarks, and when he finished one and all walked up, put on the blue ribbon and signed the pledge. Both Pete Browning and Ramsey put down their signature with good grace, and they mean to keep their word." Not only that, but "after Browning had taken the temperance pledge he went off with Manager Jim Hart and swore off before a magistrate. He wanted it done officially. Hart has great influence over him."[55] (Recall Hart had been the Louisville manager prior to Kelly's appointment. Hart was in Louisville at the time with his current team, Milwaukee, for an exhibition series.)

Sad to say, Pete Browning's story did not have a happy ending. Nor did his team play the brilliant baseball many predicted after all the men swore off liquor. In a case of cruel irony, in 1888, Louisville had its worst season in years, finishing seventh place with a 48-87 mark. It was not a surprise, therefore, when players started weakening and backsliding on their pledge, Browning among them. By June, on the road in Kansas City, he was so intoxicated that when it rained one day, he bought two fishing poles and proceeded to fish the water flowing through the gutters. Unsuccessful at urban fishing, he went inside the team hotel and acted so obnoxiously that hotel management removed him from the premises, nearly calling for his arrest, so he could sober up in the drunk tank. Realizing Browning was useless in his present state, the team left him in Kansas City when it moved on to Cincinnati for its next set of games. A Louisville sportswriter noted, "Since then nothing has been heard of him, but he is expected to telegraph for permission to join the club as soon as he gets sober."[56] By August, things were so bad he was still at home in Louisville while the team took to the road. He was drunk frequently, and he passed his time throwing poker dice.[57] He even made a September trip to French Lick Springs, "an Indiana resort much patronized by people who wish to boil out," but even that did not help. The same writer stated, "He has been back two or three days, but if reports are to be credited another boiling out is already necessary."[58]

Ramsey's 1888 season likewise ended on a down note. On June 28, the Colonels suspended him without pay because, like Browning, he had commenced drinking at the end of the Kansas City series and was in no condition to play.[59] A few weeks later, he landed in jail because various bartenders to whom he owed money pooled their complaints and had him locked up for failing to pay his bills. Because Ramsey had already missed the team's train earlier in the week, and the team had laid him off without pay for the transgression, the left-hander remained incarcerated for the time being.[60] Saddest of all, considering that Ramsey's pay for the 1888 season was $2,000, "he was unable to give bonds and spent the night in jail. As he was utterly penniless he was the next day allowed to take the insolvent debtors' oath and was released. His entire earthly possessions consisted of the clothes he wore. None of the club officials went near him and he even had to borrow $5 to pay court costs."[61]

Ramsey's incarceration produced a mixed reaction on the part of the Louisville faithful. Some pointed out the obvious truth that Ramsey tended to lose control of himself and behave in ways detrimental to himself and the Colonels. However, because of his talent, the team usually gave him another chance, and so this time, he was only seeing the consequences of his actions, as he should have done long ago. Others, more charitable, pointed out that Ramsey's patronage of the saloons in question had made the saloonkeepers many times the amount of money Ramsey owed them through his magnetism and ability to draw patrons to their establishments in the first place. Furthermore, what they had done was probably not legal anyway because Kentucky state law at the time allowed for the arrest of debtors only if they planned to leave the state without paying their debts, which Ramsey clearly did not intend to do for any greater period than the length of the team's next road trip.[62]

The two men signed again to play with the Colonels for 1889 because new owner Mordecai Davidson did not learn the lessons that should have been obvious by now. Ramsey and Browning had so much talent, however, that the temptation to keep them around was just too great. As Davidson said of Browning, "If that man would keep sober he would be the greatest ball player living. He has the best eye for a ball that I ever saw, and unless he is drunk on the grounds his playing is not affected, not even by a spree the night before. I expect trouble with him, but I will stand no foolishness." When it came time to sign Browning for 1889, "Pete's arm dropped to his vest pocket, and after much struggling he flushed out a carefully folded document, which he exhibited with much satisfaction to his employer. The paper was a pledge of total abstinence good from date until November 1, and was duly witnessed, signed, and sworn to before a neighboring Justice of the Peace." Davidson could not help a little laugh at the "unique document" but nonetheless gave Browning a contract.[63]

Browning's erratic behavior made it difficult to believe he really intended to break his habit, and he always fell short of his goal. At least he tried to start the 1889 season on the right foot. Ramsey did not even make it to Opening Day in 1889 before deciding to skip practice and vanish: "He did not reappear for three days, and, although he put on a bold front at first, it was easily seen that he had been drinking."[64] Finally, Louisville management tired of his continual lushing and traded him to the St. Louis Browns during the season for one of the Browns' recalcitrant pitchers, Nat Hudson. As sad as Ramsey's saga is, however, it is worth noting that by 1889, even after several seasons of frequent binge drinking, he was still a mere twenty-four years old. He was not the first person of that age to struggle with alcohol abuse. When the alcoholic is a major league baseball player, however, the consequences are public and the fall from grace harder than it is for those operating outside the spotlight of professional sports.

Nonetheless, the story of Ramsey and Browning demonstrates beyond any doubt just how detrimental drinking was in this era. It did much to ruin Ramsey's career because he was out of baseball by age twenty-six. Certainly, nothing was wrong with his arm. His last major league season, 1889, saw him pitch 328 innings and lead the American Association in strikeouts per nine innings. Browning lasted longer but missed so many games due to drinking and the resulting suspensions that despite a monstrous career batting mark of .341/.403/.467, he is not in the Hall of Fame simply because he did not play enough to accumulate sufficient statistics. His career also ended somewhat prematurely, at age 33. The quality of his play is certainly high enough for the Hall of Fame—his batting average is one of the best in baseball history for a player not in the Hall, but it is hard to make much of an argument on behalf of a player so completely unreliable. The fact that Louisville depended for success on two such unreliable players helps explain why the team was so streaky in the 1880s and why it performed so poorly in 1888 and 1889. This, in turn, helps demonstrate why some baseball owners stressed nonstop about alcohol and why they took such stringent measures against it.

Occasionally, a team manager attempted to do the impossible and field an entire team of sober, reliable players. When the Washington Nationals joined the National League in 1886, no one expected the team to do very well. It did not. In fact, manager Mike Scanlon's nine was a pathetic 28-92 during the '86 campaign. It wasn't all Scanlon's fault, however. Due to the financial rules of the day governing when a team might sign players from minor league teams, other major league teams had signed four of his best men, pitcher Abner Powell, catcher Chris Fulmer, infielder Bill White, and utility player Buster Hoover, immediately following the 1885 season. Only then, after these quality performers departed, had the National League extended membership to the Nationals. So, when Scanlon looked around for something positive to say about his team's chances for 1886, he settled on the moral habits of his men when trying to drum up enthusiasm for baseball in the nation's capital.

When an interviewer asked Scanlon about his club's chances prior to the 1886 campaign, Scanlon wasted no time in pointing out that "some people don't understand players, but I will have one thing in favor of my team; they are all temperate men and do not need to be shadowed."[65] Scanlon would know; as the prosperous former owner of a pool hall, he had certainly seen what drinking could do to someone.[66] As noted, the Nationals did not win many games that year, but at least lost while putting their best foot forward.

Things had changed by the following season, however. The club revamped its roster and brought in several new players, and these changes brought vast improvement on the field. The team won eighteen more games in 1887 than it had the year before, although it started from such a low level that even such tremendous improvement left it in seventh place with a 46-76 record. The performance gains came at a price, however. One Washington writer stated, "The list of absolutely sober players on the Washington team is said, by local papers, to be even smaller than *The Sporting Life* conjectured. Hines, Mack and Gilmore are the only ones who can honestly claim clean skirts this season." Seeing that *The Sporting Life* only believed the team had four teetotalers, however, the disagreement was not so very great.[67]

The team's supporters cringed, therefore, when during the 1887-1888 off-season it appeared the club might continue moving in the wrong direction, sobriety-wise. The club signed Pat Deasley and Gid Gardner as bench players that winter, and both men arrived with a great deal of baggage:

> Washingtonians who take an interest in base ball and keep posted regarding the playing abilities of the various members of the League, do not appear to appreciate the report that the home management has secured Tom Deasley and Gid Gardner. These two men are said to be first-class ball players, when they are in condition, but unfortunately they have the reputation throughout the profession of being addicted to habits which even an oath before a magistrate could not, so it is said, control. Washington can not be made an inebriate asylum for players of that character, after the experiences of last season.[68]

The club did at least sign Deasley to a special contract in which Deasley agreed the team would withhold $1,000 of the pay due him until the end of the season. Only if he walked the straight path would the club pay him this reserved sum.[69] In Gardner's case, the team hoped it could count on him because he had stayed clean for the past year, according to a Boston sportswriter who had observed Gardner's play. The writer believed, "Gardner is a splendid second baseman or outfielder. He is not the man that he was in Baltimore."[70] With Baltimore in 1885 Gardner managed to hit a mere .218, a letdown to the cranks there. Out of the majors in 1886, he was even worse during his brief stint with Indianapolis in 1887, finishing with a .175 mark. As it turned out, Gardner played just two games with Washington in 1888, his last major league season, so the cranks at Washington's Swampdoodle Grounds did not suffer too much angst on Gardner's account. They did, however, suffer through a miserable batting performance from Deasley, who hit .157 with one extra base hit and two walks in 127 at bats. It was also Deasley's last year in the majors.

Like Scanlon's Nationals of 1886, the 1887 New York Metropolitans were not a good team, but they did take strong preventative measures against boozing: "The Mets are a strictly temperance team. . . . All the players must understand that the first offense will be punished by a heavy fine, and, if this has no effect the player or players will be blacklisted, although judging from the present make-up of the team no such harsh measures are anticipated, the discordant element having been eliminated long ago."[71] The only question mark for the Metropolitans was one of their outfielders, Chief Roseman. He had been a fine hitter in 1884 and 1885 before falling off badly in 1886, so before the 1887 season, the team almost decided to part ways with him. Metropolitans' management wanted a temperate nine, and because Roseman owned a saloon, his association with alcohol worried the team.[72] They did end up keeping him one more season, although given his poor performance in 1887, they probably should have kept to their original plan.

The experience of the Metropolitans stands in stark contrast to that of the Philadelphia Athletics of the American Association. Of all the teams in 1880s baseball, the Athletics probably lushed the hardest and most consistently and often did so in plain view of the public. Nearly every year in the second half of the decade, they were someone's popular pick to dethrone the St. Louis Browns as the Association's premier team, yet the Athletics never got closer to first place than ten games back when they finished third in 1888. This caused various writers covering the team to analyze the team's player transactions based on how each move might improve the team's overall sobriety level.

For instance, in 1885, *The Sporting Life*'s Philadelphia correspondent discussed the impact of potential personnel moves as follows: "It may be that Louisville's brilliant young short stop, McLaughlin, may be released to the Athletics. This fine player would amply replace Houck, as he is a good short stop with none of Houck's bad habits." Similarly, "It is quite likely that a deal will be made with Providence for Farrell, the crack second baseman, who would strengthen the club in a place where it has always been weak. This engagement would provide against the contingency of Bastian's retirement." Charlie Bastian was considering retirement because "the latter has gone into the liquor business down town with his brother-in-law and is doing such good business that he is reported as saying that he will not play ball next season. He doesn't care much about playing second base anyhow, and feels disgruntled over a couple of fines which were imposed upon him last season and were deducted from his pay."[73]

This problem stalked the Athletics constantly. By 1888, their management had assembled a good team with many quality players, especially at bat. Between Henry Larkin at first base, Lou Bierbauer at second, Denny Lyons at third, and outfielders Harry Stovey and Curt Welch, the Athletics managed to lead the American Association in OPS, finishing ten points better than Association champion St. Louis and at least twenty-six points better than any other club. Stovey was one of baseball's greatest players. Contemporaries lauded his hitting, baserunning, defense, and gentlemanly deportment. Yet, despite high expectations, the team finished in third place in 1888. Granted, the Browns put up an excellent record, but that was little consolation to the Athletics' faithful. This finish was even more disappointing when news leaked out of the lushing tendencies of five Athletic players.

When the club visited Cincinnati that year, these five men, already with questionable reputations in Philadelphia itself, lost no time in showing the denizens of Cincinnati their true colors. Cincinnati management grimaced, too, when one of their own men, catcher Kid Baldwin, joined the Athletics in their patronage of local saloons. As one Cincinnati newspaper reported,

> No man can drink whiskey and play base ball and make a success of both. . . . There is one team in the American Association that but for the bibulous inclination of its members would stand an elegant opportunity of winning the championship. This team is now well up in the race, but would be higher did the members not worship at the shrine of Bacchus. It is a grand aggregation of boozers, and, during their last visit to this city the members had on large-sized packages of Over-the-Rhine product most of the time. Several times one or two of the players came on the field 'feeling rather happy.' A player must be rather far gone when he can't wait until after the game to get a drink. This was the case with two of the members of the team in question. While a game was in progress these players marched boldly up to a bar in their uniforms and tossed off two and three bowls of the amber.[74]

The team's manager in 1888, Billy Sharsig, apparently was aware of the problem, but for whatever reason, he was loath to discipline his men. While the problems continued when the Athletics reached Louisville, an event in St. Louis was probably the low point of the season, in terms of sobriety: "Not satisfied with going around 'lushing' at night time, President Von der Ahe charges them with bringing a keg of beer to the grounds on July 4." Chris Von der Ahe, owner of the St. Louis Browns, claimed, "I went up to where the Athletics were and saw that they had a keg of beer there. Seeing that none of my men were around I came back and told Sharsig of what I saw. Sharsig wanted me to have the keg removed.

I told him it was none of my business what his players did and if he wanted the keg emptied he should empty it himself." It is a testament to the talent level of the Athletics that even though several Athletics got started a little early in celebrating the nation's independence, Von der Ahe finished his story by remarking, "Well, my players saw what was going on and they were happy, as they thought they were going to have an easy thing of it that afternoon. I was never so mad in my life as I was after that game. To think that we were beaten by a lot of drunken ball players riled me and I felt like selling out and quitting the business."[75]

The drinking escapades of major league players cost teams games on the field, no doubt. The careers of men like Tom Ramsey and Pete Browning also illustrate that because there are never enough talented players to go around, even men with a weakness for drink might receive plentiful second chances. Sometimes teams saw no choice but to swallow hard, take the plunge, and hope things turned out for the best. Louisville did every year, and other clubs sometimes did the same, especially when they were as poor as the 1886 Kansas City Cowboys and had little to lose. Wallowing with a record of 19 up and 52 down, on August 11, the Cowboys brought Frank Ringo on board to catch: "It is to be hoped that he will brace up and play good ball, inasmuch as this is his home; however, Mr. McKim informs me that they will stand no lushing whatever, and upon his first disregard of this strict rule he will be heavily fined."[76] As it turned out, Ringo was not the answer that the Cowboys hoped for. Though he posted tolerable batting stats in limited action, and observers labeled him "a very active player, and the best throwing catcher we have,"[77] the team lost nine straight after his signing and won just eleven more games the rest of the season.

We should not forget, however, that sometimes players who could not control their drinking ruined their lives as well as their careers, and the coda to Ringo's time in Kansas City demonstrates one such story. The team let him go at the end of the 1886 campaign, "his greatest enemy being the sole reason. Frank had done excellently until he struck St. Louis, where he forgot his former resolutions, and began getting drunk which caused Manager Rowe's prompt action."[78] Like so many other men prone to strong drink, he spent the winter of 1886-1887 looking for a new club while claiming sobriety. It did not work, and he made no further appearances in major league baseball. These circumstances forced him to spend the winter as a traveling cigar salesperson for West & Co., operating out of Kansas City.[79] He seems to have had reasonable success in this line of work, but apparently, it was not satisfactory to him. In April of 1889, "after eight months of total abstinence he began drinking about two weeks ago and has continued it ever since." He even married as he tried to keep his life in order, but tragically, on April 12, 1889, Ringo killed himself.[80] The next day, the *Chicago Daily Tribune* reported, "Frank M. Ringo, the well-known ball-player, who took forty grains of morphine yesterday morning with suicidal intent, died at 9 o'clock this morning."[81]

Alcoholism also contributed to the death of Lew Brown, a promising catcher who, sadly, could not shake his need for intoxicating liquors. In 1886, Brown found his name on baseball's blacklist because he signed to play with a minor league team in New York, and the team advanced him some money, but Brown never showed up to join the team.[82] Perhaps it was fate catching up to him, or just the alcohol, but by 1889 Brown was dead. He broke his kneecap in a wrestling match and died from complications from the injury after a doctor amputated his leg and pneumonia set in.[83] One source reported he broke his kneecap not from wrestling itself but when the owner of the drinking establishment he worked for struck him with a gas pipe for a refusal to stop wrestling.[84] Whatever the truth, Brown's problems, like those of so many Gilded Age ballplayers, stemmed from his long and intimate association with liquor. Several writers remarked on his abilities and friendly disposition when in proper form and free of demon rum, and most appeared saddened at his death: "If Brownie had let booze alone no catcher would have compared with him. His backstopping was marvelous. All deliveries were the same to him. He handled them all with equal ease. A more good hearted, white souled fellow never lived. Peace unto his ashes."[85]

The story of Charlie Sweeney provides one final example of how drink could sabotage not only the career of a highly promising player, but his entire life as well. In 1883, the California team employing him expelled him from their club for "dishonorable conduct" in a May 13 game and called for Sweeney's blacklisting. However, his next team, Providence of the National League, claimed Sweeney's dismissal from the California club was a frame job, so it could avoid potential criticism and secure Sweeney's considerable talents.[86] It did not take long for them to tire of Sweeney's antics, however. By mid-1884, despite an impeccable pitching effort (an ERA+ of 183 for Providence) he was with St. Louis of the Union Association. When that team moved to the National League in 1885, Sweeney disgraced himself by sucker punching teammate Emmett Seery in the team's clubhouse. This caused the *St. Louis Critic* to state, "It is very doubtful if Sweeney will ever play ball in St. Louis again. . . . Seery is a little gentleman, while Sweeney is a whiskey-guzzling, cowardly nincompoop. His cowardly treachery . . . brands Sweeney as a cur, and we sincerely trust that Mr. Lucas will give him his release."[87] Seery, in marked contrast to his assailant, burnished his standing as a gentleman by gaining a reputation as one of baseball's premier chess players.[88] Rather than release such a talented player, however, Lucas gave the pitcher one more chance in 1886, after Sweeney pledged to mend his ways: "Charley Sweeney is said to have reformed. He has not yet joined the Salvation Army, but is said to leave liquor severely alone, and is trying hard to get into good playing shape. If he succeeds he will again try his hand in St. Louis."[89] Things did not work out, however, and Sweeney only pitched in eleven games in the Mound City.

Sweeney pitched just one more, highly ineffective, season in the majors. He threw his last pitch in major league baseball at age twenty-four. Released by the minor league Syracuse Stars late in 1886, Sweeney's career bottomed out so quickly that *The Sporting Life* lamented his fall from glory: "Alas, what a drop for a pitcher who in '84 was considered the finest of them all. On Tuesday last he pitched for the Constableville Club against the Lowvilles."[90] *The Sporting News*, describing Sweeney's Syracuse performance, concurred: "Charley Sweeney . . . was no stronger here and has been given his release. He pitched a slow, straight ball which the opposing clubs had no difficulty in hitting."[91] He finished the season with the Sacramento Altas in his native California.

Although his time as a quality major league pitcher was over after 1886, Sweeney was talented enough that the Cleveland Blues gave him a shot as a utility player for 1887, mainly manning first base and the outfield, but Sweeney never could shake his taste for liquor. Even his 1887 marriage to a Sacramento woman could not get him to settle down.[92] When a touring team of major league players visited California in December of 1887, he brandished a Colt revolver at New York Giant first baseman Roger Connor "with true Western enthusiasm, and though prevented from increasing the Coroner's troubles kept up the feud and expressed a wild desire for blood."[93] At age thirty-two, Sweeney killed a man in a saloon, resulting in incarceration. He died shortly after his release, in California, at the age of thirty-eight.[94]

On other occasions, the consequences of drinking, while not fatal, were almost as disastrous, as in the case of Frank Larkin (also known as Terry Larkin), a man who pitched with several teams between 1876 and 1880. Late in 1883, Larkin, while under the influence, shot his wife, Catherine, at their home in Brooklyn because she got on his case for coming home drunk again. His wife's screams attracted the attention of a passing police officer, but when the officer investigated, Larkin shot at him as well. He then cut his own throat with a razor blade and lay down to die, but the policeman, reinforced by some fellow officers, forced his way into Larkin's home and saved both people from death. After recovering at the hospital and regretting what he had done to his wife, fearing that she would still die, he despaired and again unsuccessfully attempted suicide, this time by gashing his head against a steam register. Bystanders restrained him before he completed the act, despite his plea, "for God's sake hit me in the head and put an end to my suffering."[95]

Larkin, out of incarceration but still battling to stay sober, played forty games as a second baseman for the Richmond Virginians, a team that played a partial season in the American Association, in 1884. Out of the game in 1885, however, he took a job that was probably a poor choice, given his history with booze: bartending in Brooklyn. Early in 1886, Larkin's employer discharged him, and in his anger, Larkin went home to arm himself, then stormed back into the saloon with two loaded pistols and challenged his boss, James McAnany, to a duel. Fortunately, while Larkin marched off the requisite paces, McAnany saw an opportunity and slipped out the back door and hailed a policeman, which resulted in Larkin's reincarceration, awaiting trial while he sobered up.[96]

Following this sad episode, Larkin checked himself into the Inebriates Home at Fort Hamilton. It seems his love of baseball was almost as strong as his love of alcohol, leading one writer to report, "During the entire six months he hasn't touched a drop of liquor, and it is thought that he has now entirely conquered his weakness. He has still many friends in Brooklyn who would like to see him get a position with a minor league club, in order that he may show the profession that he has redeemed himself."[97] Larkin even penned a short article that appeared in *The Sporting Life* in January of 1887, attempting to repair some of the damage to his reputation. He claimed "that I have reformed for good and all, no more to be the 'most gorgeous drunk' of the age" and that his arm was right once again. He hoped for one more chance to play, but that chance was not forthcoming from any major league team.[98]

What should be clear by this point is that almost every major league team, and those in the American Association above all, had problems virtually every year with some of their men drinking. No team was safe from this danger unless it kept up ceaseless vigilance, and even fines, special contracts, and suspensions were not always enough to ensure sobriety. Players might lay off from booze and rehabilitate themselves for a year, only to fall back into old ways the next. At times, managers must have felt as if they were running in sand going uphill. They had to try something to deal with the drinking, however, or else risk the fate of the Philadelphia Athletics or Louisville Colonels, forever doomed to underachieving performances. Their efforts to control the drinking behavior of their players, as we shall see, produced mixed results both on and off the field.

---

[1] "Notes and Comments," *The Sporting Life*, January 13, 1886, 3. Sportswriters did not always sign their articles in the 1880s, and sometimes used initials or pen names as well, so we cannot always know the identity of each writer with certainty.

[2] O. P. Caylor, "Caylor's Comment," *The Sporting Life*, November 30, 1887, 2. Oliver Perry Caylor was one of the most insightful and well-informed sportswriters of the day. When he kept his sarcasm within reasonable limits, he was also among the most entertaining. He also served as the manager of both the Red Stockings and the New York Metropolitans at various points in the 1880s, and helped found the American Association in 1882.

[3] "Our New Browns," *The Sporting News*, December 3, 1887, 1.

[4] "Notes and Comments," *The Sporting Life*, January 13, 1886, 3.

[5] Please see the appendix on statistics for an explanation if any of the statistics used in this book are unfamiliar.

[6] "Caught on the Fly," *The Sporting News*, August 9, 1886, 5.

[7] "Caught on the Fly," *The Sporting News*, August 30, 1886, 5.

[8] "Caught on the Fly," *The Sporting News*, December 4, 1886, 3.

[9] "Notes and Comments," *The Sporting Life*, October 5, 1887, 6.

[10] "Caught on the Fly," *The Sporting News*, October 22, 1887, 4.

[11] "Notes and Comments," *The Sporting Life*, April 4, 1888, 5.

[12] Cincinnatus, "Cincinnati's Giants," *The Sporting News*, March 17, 1886, 7.

[13] Cincinnatus, "The Coming Champions," *The Sporting News*, March 29, 1886, 6.

[14] O .P. Caylor, "Caylor's Letter," *The Sporting Life*, April 28, 1886, 1.

[15] "Notes and Comments," *The Sporting Life*, March 24, 1886, 3. Comments on a pitcher's "speed" refer to their velocity when pitching the ball. Barnie was Billy Barnie, manager of the Baltimore franchise. To avoid confusion, however, note that in the nineteenth century, the manager of the team was more of a businessman than a game manager. Most decisions regarding game strategy came from the team captain.

[16] "Notes and Comments," *The Sporting Life*, November 18, 1885, 3.

[17] "Notes and Comments," *The Sporting Life*, August 18, 1886, 5.

[18] "Caught on the Fly," *The Sporting News*, August 23, 1886, 5.

[19] "Caught on the Fly," *The Sporting News*, September 20, 1886, 5.

[20] Pritchard, "From St. Louis," *The Sporting Life*, January 5, 1887, 2.

[21] "Notes and Comments," *The Sporting Life*, January 12, 1887, 3.

[22] "Notes and Comments," *The Sporting Life*, March 9, 1887, 3.

[23] T. T. T., "From Baltimore," *The Sporting Life*, February 16, 1887, 4. TTT was the pen name of Baltimore sportswriter Albert Mott.

[24] Jake, "Billy Taylor," *The Sporting News*, March 5, 1887, 1.

[25] "Notes and Comments," *The Sporting Life*, October 24, 1888, 2.

[26] Circle, "Pittsburg Pencilings," *The Sporting Life*, September 25, 1889, 2.

[27] J. H. B., "Billy Taylor's Disgraceful Conduct," *The Sporting News*, August 3, 1889, 1. Being "in the points" was an expression of the day that simply meant someone was the pitcher.

[28] "Intemperate Players," *The Sporting Life*, November 18, 1885, 3.

[29] F. W. Arnold, "The Baby Berated," *The Sporting Life*, May 22, 1889, 2.

[30] Ibid.

[31] "Catcher Earle Fined," *The Sporting News*, May 25, 1889, 1.

[32] "Baseball Notes," *New York Times*, November 13, 1887, 16.

[33] "Disgraceful Scenes at the New Orleans Ball Grounds," *Chicago Daily Tribune*, November 3, 1887, 6. A crank was another word

for a fan or spectator. See the appendix on terminology for this or other unfamiliar terms of nineteenth-century baseball.

[34] Plain Talk, "Manager Morrill Gives the Boston Beauty a Severe Lecture," *The Sporting News*, July 14, 1888, 1.

[35] "Kelly to Give Up Drinking," *The Sporting News*, July 21, 1888, 1.

[36] "Mike Kelly's Views," *The Sporting News*, July 21, 1888, 1.

[37] J. A., "Louisville Laconics," *The Sporting Life*, January 4, 1888, 4; Joe Pritchard, "St. Louis Siftings," *The Sporting Life*, May 9, 1888, 4.

[38] David Nemec, *The Beer and Whiskey League: The Illustrated History of the American Association—Baseball's Renegade Major League*, (New York: Lyons & Burford, 1994): 68.

[39] J. A., "Louisville Recovering," *The Sporting Life*, July 24, 1889, 3. John L. Sullivan was boxing's heavyweight champion at the time.

[40] Pritchard, "From St. Louis," *The Sporting Life*, November 24, 1886, 2; X. X., "Browning Surrenders," *The Sporting Life*, April 13, 1887, 1.

[41] "The Falls City," *The Sporting News*, March 17, 1886, 3.

[42] "Falls City News," *The Sporting Life*, March 17, 1886, 1.

[43] R. W. L., "Pete Browning at the Springs," *The Sporting News*, August 2, 1886, 1. The Louisville club of 1886 certainly was a streaky team. Between July 4 and August 22 it won twenty-seven games against just eight defeats. The rest of the season, however, they mustered just six victories while losing thirty times. According to observers, a combination of alcohol and injuries were the reason for this incredible rollercoaster performance.

[44] Charles Alexander, *Turbulent Seasons: Baseball in 1890-1891*, (Dallas: SMU University Press, 2011): 36.

[45] Rat, "From the Falls City," *The Sporting Life*, August 18, 1886, 5.

[46] R. W. L., "Manager Hart Bounced," *The Sporting News*, September 27, 1886, 1.

[47] R. W. L., "The Falls City," *The Sporting News*, September 6, 1886, 1.

[48] Henry Chadwick, "Chadwick's Chat," *The Sporting Life*, April 27, 1887, 7.

[49] X. X. X., "From the Falls City," *The Sporting Life*, April 27, 1887, 5.

[50] Pritchard, "From St. Louis," *The Sporting Life*, January 19, 1887, 2.

[51] "Notes and Comments," *The Sporting Life*, April 20, 1887, 11; R. W. L., "Browning and the Reporters," *The Sporting News*, May 7, 1887, 1.

[52] X. X., "From the Falls City," *The Sporting Life*, September 7, 1887, 4.

[53] J. A., "From the Falls City," *The Sporting Life*, October 19, 1887, 5.

[54] J. A., "From the Falls City," *The Sporting Life*, October 12, 1887, 4.

[55] J. A., "Louisville Laconics," *The Sporting Life*, April 25, 1888, 3.

[56] J. A., "Louisville Laconics," *The Sporting Life*, June 27, 1888, 2.

[57] J. A., "Louisville Laconics," *The Sporting Life*, September 5, 1888, 5.

[58] J. A., "Louisville Laconics," *The Sporting Life*, September 19, 1888, 3.

[59] J. A., "Ramsey Suspended," *The Sporting Life*, July 4, 1888, 2.

[60] P. S. C., "In a Dungeon Cell," *The Sporting News*, July 28, 1888, 1.

[61] "Louisville Lines," *The Sporting Life*, August 1, 1888, 1.

[62] J. A., "Louisville Laconics," *The Sporting Life*, August 8, 1888, 5.

[63] Colonel, "Outfielder Pete Browning," *The Sporting News*, April 13, 1889, 1.

[64] Ibid.

[65] W. U. D., "From the Capital," *The Sporting Life*, March 17, 1886, 3. W. U. D. was the pen name of Washington sportswriter R. H. Wood. He wrote for *The Sporting Life* until 1887 when, surprisingly given the ghastly treatment of major league umpires in the 1880s, he gave up writing and attempted to become an umpire. This did not go as planned, however, and by July of 1888, he was a minor league manager instead.

[66] Nemec, *The Beer and Whiskey League*, 79.

[67] "Notes and Comments," *The Sporting Life*, October 5, 1887, 6; W. U. D., "From the Capital," *The Sporting Life*, October 5, 1887, 7.

[68] Bob Larner, "The Hines Deal," *The Sporting Life*, November 23, 1887, 1. Deasley's given name was Thomas, but he went by Pat while playing ball.

[69] S. A. M., "Spalding on Pfeffer" *The Sporting News*, November 26, 1887, 5.

[70] Henry Chadwick, "Chadwick's Chat," *The Sporting Life*, December 21, 1887, 3.

[71] Regular, "New York Gossip," *The Sporting Life*, March 2, 1887, 4.

[72] Regular, "The Mets," *The Sporting Life*, February 2, 1887, 1. I have been unable to determine if Roseman was an American Indian, but it seems possible, given that "Chief" was a common nickname given to American Indians who played major league baseball in this era. Although Roseman was born in Brooklyn, and died there, too, there is an interesting, although rather racist, statement about him in 1887 which reads, "It's dollars to cents that Jimmy Roseman will not lift his stentorian war whoop for the Mets next season. Alas, even like unto his brother, the noble red man of the boundless West, he and his confreres pass away." "Notes and Comments" *The Sporting Life*, February 2, 1887, 3.

[73] "The Local Clubs," *The Sporting Life*, December 2, 1885, 1.

[74] "Philadelphia Pointers," *The Sporting Life*, September 5, 1888, 6.

[75] "Philadelphia Pointers," *The Sporting Life*, September 5, 1888, 6.

[76] L. J. K., "Kansas City News," *The Sporting Life*, August 18, 1886, 1.

[77] L. J. K., "From Cowboy Town," *The Sporting Life*, September 22, 1886, 1.

[78] L. J. K., "Kansas City News," *The Sporting Life*, October 13, 1886, 1.

[79] "Notes and Comments," *The Sporting Life*, March 2, 1887, 3.

[80] Freeman, "Kansas City Briefs," *The Sporting Life*, April 17, 1889, 1.

[81] "Catcher Frank M. Ringo Dead," *Chicago Daily Tribune*, April 13, 1889, 6.

[82] "Notes and Comments," *The Sporting Life*, August 4, 1886, 5.

[83] Mugwump, "Hub Happenings," *The Sporting Life*, January 23, 1889, 4; "Lew Brown Dead," *The Sporting Life*, January 23, 1889, 4.

[84] T. H. M., "John Morrill Happy," *The Sporting News*, February 9, 1889, 3.

[85] A. G. Merwin, "The Boston Club," *The Sporting News*, February 2, 1889, 3.

[86] "The League," *The Sporting Life*, June 24, 1883, 2.

[87] "The Sweeney-Seery Fight," *The Sporting Life*, November 25, 1885, 3.

[88] "Notes and Comments," *The Sporting Life*, March 9, 1887, 3.

[89] "Notes and Comments," *The Sporting Life*, February 24, 1886, 4.

[90] "Notes and Comments," *The Sporting Life*, August 4, 1886, 5. Constableville and Lowville are actual towns in the Empire State, but their caliber of baseball was not what Sweeney's previous baseball exploits seemed to warrant. He lost the game, 4-0.

[91] S. U. T., "Sweeney Again Fired," *The Sporting News*, August 2, 1886, 1.

[92] Wally Wallace, "From California," *The Sporting Life*, March 16, 1887, 3.

[93] "Ball-Tossers on the Slope," *Chicago Daily Tribune*, December 20, 1887, 3.

[94] David Stevens, *Baseball's Radical for All Seasons: A Biography of John Montgomery Ward*, (Lanham, MD: Scarecrow Press, 1998): 37.

[95] "Larkin Again in Trouble," *The Sporting Life*, January 20, 1886, 2; Bill James, *The New Bill James Historical Baseball Abstract: The Classic—Completely Revised*, (New York: The Free Press, 2001): 51.

[96] "Larkin Again in Trouble," *The Sporting Life*, January 20, 1886, 2.

[97] "News and Notes," *The Sporting Life*, January 5, 1887, 3.

[98] Frank Larkin, "Larkin Speaks for Himself," *The Sporting Life*, January 26, 1887, 5.

Chapter 2

Limiting Alcohol Abuse

Gilded Age ballplayers were, collectively, a rather dissolute lot. Their tendency to drink too much cost their teams games on the field and sabotaged many potentially fine careers. Probably the only reason that drinking did not hurt teams worse than it did is that their opponents often drank just as much, so the negative costs of the drinking canceled each other out. This led some observers, team owners and managers especially, to question whether, if they could only keep their hometown nine in a sober condition, they might gain an advantage on the competition.

From management's point of view, more was at stake with the drinking issue than just wins and losses, however. It is easy to forget that in the 1880s, baseball and the idea of team sports was still a new feature of the United States sporting landscape. The idea of operating a professional sports league based on the profit motive was a relatively recent innovation. That meant that baseball needed to establish itself in the public mind and do so in a way that invited public confidence. The big issue of the 1870s had been gambling. Baseball's leaders had to work hard to clear out the gambling element and make the public believe in the integrity of their sport.

Several crooked players ended up banned from the game for life as a result. By the 1880s, gambling might threaten to rear its ugly head here and there, but for the most part, that crisis was over. The last thing baseball owners wanted to see was an issue like drinking threaten the game the way gambling had.

They had still other reasons for wanting to make sure that players stayed as sober as possible. Many owners, led by Al Spalding of the Chicago White Stockings, feared that having players with poor morals might keep fans away from the ballpark, especially middle-class fans. These people tended to buy the more expensive tickets and have more money to spend generally, and owners such as Spalding thought the game should cater to them whenever possible. This was especially true in National League cities like Chicago, where tickets in the bleachers cost fifty cents and grandstand tickets seventy-five. If, however, these middle-class spectators thought they were watching a game played by a group of drunken boors, and played poorly at that because the players drank too much, they would spend their entertainment money elsewhere and stay away from baseball. Spalding summed up this approach thusly:

> There are two classes of the patrons of professional baseball grounds which club Presidents and Directors have their choice in catering to for each season, and these are, first, the reputable class, who prefer to see the game played scientifically and by gentlemanly exemplars of the beauties of the game; and second, the hoodlum element, who revel in noisy coaching, "dirty ball playing," kicking against the umpires, and exciting disputes and rows every inning. . . . But all of the clubs have not followed this example, the majority committing the blunder of considering only the tastes and requirements of the hoodlum class apparently in catering for patronage. This is a great financial mistake. Experience has shown conclusively that it pays best to cater solely for the best class of patronage. The work in doing this is

so much more satisfactory for one thing, and it is sure to be the most remunerative.[1]

These, then, were the three most important reasons team owners wanted to have sober players. Sober players meant more wins, but they also meant more public confidence in baseball and more patronage at the ballpark. As a result, team owners went to great lengths to get their men to behave themselves during the season. Drunkenness, or other forms of loutish behavior such as swearing, fighting, blatant cheating, and so forth, might alienate middle-class people and keep them away from the grounds, and teams would lose money. That is why teams felt that they must limit drinking at almost any cost.

Among the simplest and most straightforward things teams could do to reprimand drinking players was fine them for bad behavior. This, however, was trickier than it might seem on the surface. Often, players did do things to hurt their teams with their off-field behavior. It was perfectly natural that owners and managers wanted to prevent this whenever possible. They had both a competitive and financial interest in doing so. Most players, recognizing this, did not "kick" over fines imposed for obvious and blatant misconduct. A sizable gray area existed, however, between the clear incidents such as showing up drunk for a game, or going out in public with gamblers, and the petty things that teams did simply to antagonize their players by keeping them in fear and taking bites out of their salaries. Teams fined players often, and for many reasons, besides just drinking.

Part of the problem was that different teams held different standards of what was acceptable and what was not. More critically, however, the language of player contracts was very vague on what constituted a violation of team rules. The 1888 American Association contract, for instance, stipulated (Clause Two) that the player keep himself in proper moral and physical condition but did not specify what constituted the proper condition. Clause Three stated that if the player was careless, indifferent, or conducted himself in a prejudicial manner, it was a violation of the contract. The definition of any of these terms, of course, was at the discretion of the team; thus, an owner who was vindictive, avaricious, or petty, and many owners were, could use the wording of the contract to fine players for marginal, or even nonexistent, infractions and usually get away with doing so because players had no independent arbitration or appeals process.[2]

Sad to say, several team managers and owners were also in the habit of fining their players for poor play on the field, most notably the Louisville Colonels under Mordecai Davidson's putrid management in 1889. These fines, tacked on to ones for certain behaviors off the field, could add up quickly. Even though baseball players received pay that was quite respectable compared to the average worker, they understandably resented returning that pay to their employer for vague charges of misbehavior that they could not appeal.

Examples abound of how teams could stretch contract language to cover almost any situation regarding fining men on vague or questionable grounds related to behavior. For instance, consider the 1884 incident where Jerry Dorgan, outfielder and captain of the Indianapolis Hoosiers of the American Association, incurred a $10 fine "for a tendency . . . not to take any sleep during the 24 hours which composed one day."[3] In August of 1885, the National League's Providence team took a similarly tough stance towards second baseman Jack Farrell. After Farrell had used "obscene and disgusting language addressed to the audience" the Grays suspended their infielder without pay.[4]

Capricious and ill-defined as some efforts to control player behavior were, this is not to say that such efforts to improve discipline were always bogus. Drinking among players occurred with depressing frequency, and fans and sportswriters knew it. Team management did, too, whether they conceded as much to the public or the press, and here, once again, the invasiveness of management's response could alienate players. If the team came down too hard or too frequently, it risked angering both the player and any teammates who might start wondering if they were next. Go too soft, however, as manager Billy Sharsig tended to do with the Philadelphia Athletics, and the players might try to take advantage and ignore all attempts at discipline.

Jack Farrell's saga also shows how, if a player behaved poorly and drank, too, his career might become a rollercoaster. After his falling out with Providence in 1885, Farrell got a fresh start for 1886, catching on with the Philadelphia Quakers, but it was not long before he wore out his welcome in the City of Brotherly Love, for the same reasons Providence tired of him. The team decided to release him after only seventeen games after he "grossly insulted his late manager, Mr. Wright," to the extent that "the latter felt greatly annoyed at Farrell's conduct, and seriously contemplated bringing his case to the attention of the league," but Wright eventually relented after Farrell signed on with Washington, perhaps simply wishing to wash his hands of the troublesome infielder altogether and let the Nationals deal with him.[5]

Surprisingly, the Nationals appointed Farrell field captain for 1887, and for a few months, he held onto this position, but by September, the team demoted him in favor of third baseman Jim Donnelly. The reason was not poor judgment on the field but poor judgment off it. While in New York, Farrell and one teammate, reserve catcher Barney Gilligan, "engaged in a slugging match with John L. Redeye when they were booked to play." While recovering from this bender, Farrell then took French leave, not reappearing for about a week, and the loss of the team's captaincy was the predictable result. The team also suspended him for the season but later changed its mind and reinstated him.[6] At the end of the 1887 campaign, Washington parted ways with Farrell, who, despite all his capers, still claimed that the Nationals' management had it out for him: "Farrell has been released and will leave for his home in a few days. I understand that he claims that he was downed. He did it himself, and if he could have curbed his vicious habits he would be today as popular as ever, for he can play ball when he will."[7]

Farrell received his last major league engagement from Baltimore for the 1888 season. Baltimore manager Billy Barnie seemed to have a soft spot for talented men who let their bad habits get the best of them. Barnie agreed with Henry Chadwick, the great encyclopedist of baseball, who described Farrell as "one of the best second base players in the fraternity," and brought Farrell to the Monumental City for 1888. Chadwick laid out the reasons for Farrell's downfall by stating he had "sacrificed glorious opportunities for rising to the topmost round of the ladder, at the shrine of that curse of the professional fraternity—drunkenness." Chadwick also described Farrell's engagement by the Bald Eagle of Baltimore by writing, "Barnie has considerately come forward and given him a chance to recover his lost credit. . . . The question is, will he have the manliness and strength of mind to benefit by the kindly offer?"[8] Farrell did not, and it spelled the end of his major league baseball career by age thirty-one.

In addition to deciding how harshly to penalize drinking players, management had to determine if the goal should be temperance or complete prohibition. Al Spalding opted to try the second option with his Chicago club in 1886, and employed the Pinkerton detective agency to shadow his players continually over a six-week period. These detectives discovered, for instance, that one evening, third baseman Tom Burns played billiards for two hours, while shortstop Ned Williamson and first baseman Cap Anson, who was almost as good at billiards as he was at baseball, limited themselves to eighty minutes at the billiards table. Meanwhile pitcher Jim McCormick and catcher Silver Flint left their hotel with two men, enjoyed a pair of beers at a nearby bar, and then returned to the team lodgings. When the team got to Kansas City, Spalding fined the guilty parties who had been drinking. His detectives rounded up information on the after-hours behavior of players on other clubs, as well. Spalding clearly enjoyed the power this gave him, to the point where he recommended the entire National League do the same: "I shall ask the clubs of the National League to jointly arrange with some detective agency to shadow throughout the League season every player of the National League; and submit a weekly report to President Young at Washington, embracing a statement of each player's habits and of his actions from day to day."[9]

It appears some other teams liked Spalding's idea. Louisville reportedly imitated the White Stockings when trying to police the postgame behavior of its nine. Manager Jim Hart "has been watching the boys very carefully, and as a result there has been no dissipation to amount to anything. . . . Besides being under the eye of Manager James, a detective, it is reported, is constantly on their track, who takes note of the individual doings of each man and reports them in writing to President Phelps each morning." Although the players naturally chafed at this arrangement, especially those most socially inclined, the author of this piece favored the practice, stating, "In my opinion, and the opinion of a great portion of the public, it is the proper thing. Ball players are paid large salaries to play ball and they should do it well. Spectators do not pay admission to see certain men who have been carousing all night, and play in a listless manner as though they took no interest whatever in what was going on. Every club should have a detective in their ranks."[10] Over in Boston, a trio of men known as the Triumvirs ran the team, and they were listening, too. They also employed detectives to keep track of their players throughout the 1887 and 1888 seasons. Therefore, when some critics tried to blame Boston's pedestrian performance on dissipation and carousing amongst the players during the evenings, Boston's ownership put little stock in such stories.[11]

Pittsburgh also tried to enforce a no-drinking policy amongst its men for the 1889 season, but the players on the Smoky City nine were wise to management's tactics by that point. One unnamed player, who had not drunk at all in 1888, believed that going cold turkey had hurt his play, and declared he would drink in moderation in 1889, come what may. Realizing that detectives could shadow him if he went out for a drink in public, "if Manager Phillips catches him in a saloon through the season he has no doubt but that he will be fined, but he does not propose to give 'Harry' a chance, and will keep the article bottled on his own premises and has no doubt but that other players will follow his example. . . . If all the players did their drinking at home it would be next to impossible to detect any infractions."[12]

Unsurprisingly, this level of surveillance did not sit well with players, prompting some to emulate the Pittsburgh players who simply drank at home. Besides the basic reaction to the invasion of their private lives and the increased level of control their employers gained over them, these men were professionals. Even a man on good terms with ownership, such as the White Stockings' captain, Cap Anson, took umbrage with the shadowing. When his team, locked in a fierce pennant race with Detroit and New York, lost five out of six games on its August road trip to the East Coast in 1886, Anson blamed the fines administered by Spalding for disrupting the team's momentum. He did not deny what the reports of the Pinkertons revealed—he only disputed that the occasional glass of beer had hurt the team's performance in any tangible way: "It is only natural that such an act on the part of the club management, coming, as it did, in the nature of a complete surprise and then being made public, should have chagrined and displeased the men. Their defeats down East, I believe, are the result of the whole affair. Not that they have deliberately determined to lose games, mind you, but they are sore and are playing with a kind of dogged indifference." When a writer countered that Spalding's primary objective was to ascertain the truth regarding published reports of excess drinking on the part of the players, Anson conceded this might be legitimate but still held to his statement that the public nature of the discipline embarrassed a team of professionals, who now felt like unruly schoolchildren wearing dunce caps. For his part, the writer did not believe Anson's tale that the fines translated into lackluster play (perhaps for good reason because some observers then and baseball historians now considered Anson a blowhard) but chalked up the defeats to a string of bad luck instead.[13]

While infielder Ned Williamson declared his twenty-five dollar fine a steep price for a mere two beers, claiming that this was the only time so far in the season he had let down his guard against the bottle, one White Stocking, burly pitcher Jim McCormick, went further than mere complaining about having Pinkertons shadow him every evening. Just before his team boarded a train for their trip east in August, McCormick noticed one of the detectives in the train depot and decided to repay the detective for his fine by taking the money out of the man's hide: "The detective bolted, but the base ball giant was too quick, and, catching Mr. Detective by the throat, he proceeded to stop his wind. Having squeezed as long as he thought safe he threw the fellow from him, and, with a final thump in the eye and a pleasant 'ta-ta' he jumped aboard the train, which was already in motion."[14] Williamson later speculated, as Anson had, that Spalding's fines hurt the morale of the Chicago nine at a critical time in the season: "Big Ed Williamson says that together Kelly, Gore, Flint, himself and another player were fined $2,000 at the close of the season for drinking. He believes that the loss of the [World] series of games to the St. Louis Browns was the cause of punishment inflicted by the Chicago president upon these men."[15]

Unlikely as it may seem, despite the frequent mentions in the press, it is possible that writers underestimated the influence of demon rum in the game because it seems nearly every team suffered from players drinking excessively at one point or another. Despite Spalding's claims that his men never drank, many considered this claim a façade: "Ball players snicker when the wonderful sobriety of the Chicago team last season is mentioned. More than one League player is willing to swear that the champions stood up to the rack well up to July, but that after that many were the rackets and benders indulged in."[16] The actual record of the White Stockings, however, does not bear out this statement. The club won thirty-four games against eleven defeats in August, September, and October that season, and this squares well with their fifty-three wins against only fourteen losses to that point. So perhaps the accusations against them were spurious. However, it is also possible that this charge is correct, but their opponents were equally inebriated, resulting in no net loss of performance on the part of the White Stockings. Spalding, while not exactly a disinterested party, denied the report as well, stating, "They went through the season without indulging in any excess, and they deserve to receive credit for it. They seemed to take a great deal of pride in keeping themselves straight, and it would not have been good for some of the new members to have spoiled their record in this respect."[17]

The reader might wonder at the veracity of Spalding's claims, however, considering that he employed detectives to shadow those same players the subsequent season. Similarly, the critics, unconvinced by Spalding's bravado, did not relent in their accusations. One offered that, regarding Chicago catcher Silver Flint, "we are sorry to make this heinous charge, for we knew Flint in days gone by as a high-minded gentleman. . . . Now, however, we are informed that at Flint's gymnasium the growler is rushed early and often." The writer did point out that Flint's friends in St. Louis disputed these charges but only because "they, too, knew him as a high-minded gentleman, and one who took his ale fresh from the keg rather than from the vulgar growler."[18] Even team captain Cap Anson weighed in on the matter, declaring his confidence in Flint's abilities to get back in shape following an 1885 off-season in which "every time he happened to run across him at a sporting match or in the hotel rotunda, he appeared to be enjoying himself."[19]

The problem was widespread indeed, if we believe Pittsburgh Allegheny secretary A. K. Scandrett. He claimed to have signed many contracts offering players between $200 and $500 extra if they made it through the championship season without falling victim to demon rum. He also claimed he had never actually paid a single cent of this bonus money to any player, ever, because all had failed to make good on their end of the deal.[20] Likewise, when one Baltimore sportswriter put forth the idea of simply removing all drinking men from the game, in order to ensure quality play that would invite the public's confidence, he acknowledged the idea might be a tad extreme because "the result would be sure, but perhaps this would be too radical to be practical, and so many fearful examples would have to be made that the profession would dwindle to small numbers."[21]

Occasionally, team managers would attempt to revamp an entire roster to clean out the drunkards. In the 1885-1886 off-season, for instance, St. Louis Maroons manager Gus Schmelz signed several new players to his club to try to shape up the morals of his nine. One St. Louis writer praised Schmelz's effort, remarking,

> Manager Schmelz's regime is that the whiskey-heads and bums, who have brought such disgrace upon the club and upon the game in this city, are to be retired in favor of honest, hard-working, temperate and conscientious players, who will give St. Louis the best ball that is in them and behave themselves in a manner calculated to elevate themselves and their club in public estimation instead of bringing it into public disrepute, as was the case last season.[22]

While Chicago and St. Louis tried to sober up collectively, Baltimore could not boast of the same achievement. One of their writers, describing how much the club still had to improve so that it could compete in 1886, mentioned, "It is hoped by the opening of the playing season some of the lushers can be wisely replaced by material that will invite the confidence of the public; or, if the worst comes to the worst, that the management will devise a system to keep them under control. It must be confessed, however, that the latter phase of the question is not at all promising, if past experience is to be the guide."[23]

It was not to be. Instead, the club signed shortstop Sadie Houck, hoping to keep him on the straight and narrow: "Houck may be found with the Baltimore Club next season. Barnie thinks he would fill the bill capably at short field, if he will keep straight and let up on his everlasting chinning, and that Barnie says he can make him do."[24] Since Houck's other option was a yearlong suspension from his old club, the Athletics, for bad behavior, one might think he would embrace this opportunity wholeheartedly, and he had a history of doing exactly that: "The latter always plays well and behaves himself in his first season in a new town. . . . Houck now has one more opportunity to redeem himself, and we trust he will embrace it."[25] As things turned out, however, he did anything but. Houck performed miserably at the plate in his 61 games in Baltimore, preventing manager Barnie from making good on his claim. Houck compiled a .192/.216/.231 batting line for a puny OPS+ of 42, so it is unlikely that he kept straight, or even slightly crooked for that matter, although to be fair, frequent minor injuries also took their toll.

Houck disappeared from major league baseball following the next season, 1887, after an abbreviated stint of ten exceptionally ineffective games with the New York Metropolitans. The Mets took a flyer on Houck after he started the season with the Lynn club in Massachusetts because their team was awful and had nothing to lose but quickly realized Houck was not the answer.[26] After failing in New York, Houck decided to go west: "Sadie Houck has packed his gripsack and hied himself to Kansas City, and will henceforth yell with the Cowboys," who by this time were a member of the Western League after getting the boot from the National League over the winter of 1886.[27] He never resurfaced in the major leagues after that, even though he was just thirty-one years old.

No matter how many failures he had in his experiments with drinking men, the Bald Eagle of Baltimore, Billy Barnie, just could not resist giving second and third chances to some of the game's notorious drinkers. This drew constant laments from the team's correspondent for *The Sporting Life*, Albert Mott. Comparing the 1887 campaign to the disaster of 1886, when excessive tippling contributed to Baltimore's 48-87 record, "last season the team was, by comparison with former years, remarkably free from this, and the playing record was, as a consequence, much better." Baltimore improved to 77-58, a monstrous improvement, indeed. Not that all was well, because "it is not intended to assert that there was no drinking at all, for there was really too much of it, but it was a vast improvement over the steady lushing of the teams of former years. There was not a downright lusher on the team of eighty-seven." Because of this, Mott was all the more dismayed that, "there are fears now that just enough boozing element will be in the team of eighty-eight to eventually demoralize some of the youngsters. . . . Experience has shown that in the Baltimore Club, all the iron-clad and steel-rivetted contracts in the world are as so much waste paper in restraining a player who has contracted the disease of boozing."[28]

Mott's quote regarding his fears for the upcoming 1888 season referred to manager Barnie's decision to sign Jack Farrell. As noted earlier, Farrell had not demonstrated good behavior in his recent past, this being his fourth major league team in four years as a result. As usual, Barnie offered him incentives to stay sober, in the form of a $300 salary deduction the first time he failed to toe the line, but Mott did not think this precaution was enough.[29] The tragedy was that, because of its good performance in 1887, the club was beginning to regain the favor and confidence of the cranks of the Monumental City, and Mott feared all that would be lost if the team fell back into old habits on the field and off and resumed its lackluster performances of recent campaigns.[30] (Sadly, it did, posting a 57-80 record in 1888.) The 1888 season was even more critical in Baltimore because that was the year the American Association tried upgrading its ticket prices to match those of the National League, fifty cents for the bleachers and seventy-five for the grandstand. (Previously, Association tickets had been twenty-five cents for the bleachers and fifty for the grandstand.) Mott, and many other Baltimoreans, believed that if the club played no better ball and provided no improved accommodations for its patrons, it could not justify the hike in ticket prices, and fans would cease showing up at Oriole Park.[31]

It was not Farrell, however, who got in trouble first in Baltimore in 1888. That dubious distinction went to second baseman Billy Greenwood, who earned a suspension and heavy fine for excessive drinking in May. Because Greenwood had never been a premium performer to begin with, Barnie decided the team could do without Greenwood after his drinking cost them games in a series against Cleveland, stating, "Both Mr. Vonderhorst and myself talked to him, and warned him of the consequences if he was caught drinking again. He paid no attention to us and when I discovered last night that he was spreeing, I put the fine on him and it will stick." The team declared Greenwood could not resume playing with it until June 1.[32] Greenwood's turn to the dark side was very disappointing to all associated with Baltimore baseball because the previous season he had finally managed to shed his drinking reputation and had played some of the best baseball of his life.

Although Albert Mott heaped most of his scorn on the Baltimore players for their bad habits and Baltimore's management for taking them on in the first place, he recognized additional factors in play. It seemed hypocritical to Mott to tell players they must refrain from alcohol when the team sold it during games and used beer as part of its advertising to draw spectators in the first place. Yet, in the American Association, little chance of reversing this policy existed, considering that half the teams, St. Louis, Cincinnati, Baltimore, and (by 1888) Kansas City, had owners who currently or formerly owned breweries. As Mott put it, "Now, of course, a beer man may own a club without any attempt to utilize his team as a sort of nickel-plated faucet to draw beer, but it is not apt to be the case." Mott did not deny that intoxicated players hurt a team's fortunes but pointed out that intoxicated fans did, too, by scaring away the sober patrons with their obscenities and boorish behavior. Furthermore, "The outrageous assault by a Baltimore crowd on Umpire Brennan was caused by the beer-befuddled brain of one man who rushed into the field and was followed by hundreds of others. The beer riots of Cincinnati at base ball games, where the umpire is made the target of the heavy and deadly beer glasses, is common knowledge throughout the country."[33]

There seemed little chance of eliminating beer sales at games throughout the Association, but St. Louis briefly put a stop to the practice at Sportsman's Park in 1888. Owner Chris Von der Ahe decided to eliminate beer sales in the grandstand that season, hoping to avoid the opprobrium associated with intoxicated and unruly fans. Because the grandstand tickets were more expensive, and the grandstand was where middle-class patrons tended to sit, he also thought this would spare the "respectable" fans association with the working-class spectators in the bleachers. He also attempted to make his grandstand more attractive to women at the same time by creating a special section for ladies where no men could enter unless accompanied by a woman. Von der Ahe believed this combination would help bring out the "better class" of spectators for 1888.[34] He did not deny the pleasures of the amber beverage to the denizens of the bleaching boards, however, and beer sales continued in that section of Sportsman's Park.[35]

In addition to its impact on important things like attendance and public respectability, considerations involving alcohol consumption consistently figured into calculations of how much a player was worth in comparison to other players. During the early months of 1887, for example, the New York Giants were in hot pursuit of third baseman Jerry Denny, an above-average offensive player reputed to possess superior defensive skills. John Ward once said of Denny's defense, "I say unreservedly and without hesitation that he is the greatest infielder living. He never had an equal, and I do not believe this country will ever produce another one like him."[36] Denny was a member of the St. Louis Maroons, a team on the verge of expulsion from the National League. The Giants' management, including manager Jim Mutrie, hoped to avoid using their utility player, Danny Richardson, at the hot corner in 1887 because Richardson was a little light with the bat, and they thought Denny would fit their needs admirably. Not all observers believed the upgrade would truly be an upgrade, however. Graybeard baseball writer Henry Chadwick hoped the Giants would stick with Richardson because Denny "is not the equal of Richardson in qualifications which go to make up a reliable team player on the nine. . . . Dan is temperate, Denny is not: Dan has mental ability; 'head work' is not a characteristic of Denny." He saw no reason to pursue Denny, given the cost that would entail, when the team already had a reliable player on hand.[37]

Not all agreed, however, that players such as Denny were a liability simply because they liked to down a few cold ones. His teammate in St. Louis, outfielder John Cahill, stood up for Denny when the rumors spread regarding his possible sale to the Giants: "Rumors are flying thick and fast in regard to Denny's release to the New Yorks. It would be a foolish move to sell him. Where can the management find another man that will stop the hot shots that go down to third base? I'll tell you, his place cannot be filled."[38] Still, many had doubts about Denny's overall value because of his bad habits. He spent the winter of 1886-1887 "in California in such a condition from continued lushing as to do himself no credit by performances in games out there."[39] Realizing the importance of his good name, however, Denny penned his own response to these attacks, stating, "My winter in California has been spent in hard and earnest work. I have not lushed, but I am strictly temperate and shall remain so. From constant practice I have never before been in better condition, and if health favors me will play the ball of my life." To back his claims, he quoted a California newspaper praising his efforts.[40]

Denny's story also shows that player drinking was a concern not just during the playing season but in the off-season as well. At the time of all this discussion of his convivial habits, Denny was playing January and February exhibition games in California. The baseball season remained nearly three months away, and yet, teams and sportswriters obsessed over what alcohol might do to Denny's performance and reputation.

Finally, Jerry Denny's case demonstrates that observers feared the abuse of alcohol not only for the problems it could cause on the field but also because it ruined the physical condition of men who imbibed too frequently. The career of Charles "Fatty" Briody is a classic example of this. A journeyman catcher who played for seven different teams in an eight-year career, Briody, generously listed as five-foot, eight-inches and 190 pounds in official records, was so rotund that the sporting press simply called him Fatty, or sometimes "the Alderman" or "Falstaff" when it needed a synonym for fat. He was so ponderously slow, he failed to nab a single stolen base in fifty-six games in 1886, at a time when teams expected every player to be a threat to steal bases. When Briody signed on to be the backup catcher for Detroit in 1887, his modest contract called for him to receive an extra twenty-five dollars per month if he stayed pure and did not touch liquor. Up until August, "Briody promised to do this and for some time kept his word, but when the club was on their eastern trip he fell from grace, and the information reaching President Stearns' ears resulted in the extra money being withheld." Briody only saved his bacon and avoided release by the club by convincing it that while he had indeed imbibed, it was not in such quantity as to impair his play on the field.[41]

Cincinnati was yet another team that often made financial decisions with blood alcohol content levels in mind. Before the 1887 season, Clarence "Kid" Baldwin, a catcher and utility player for the Red Stockings, made a bet with team owner Aaron Stern to abstain for the entire season. Several players in 1880s baseball earned the nickname "Kid," and, contrary to what that nickname implies, not all of them were youngsters. Instead, it was a nickname earned by acting in a wild or unruly fashion on a consistent basis. In his bet, Baldwin went before a notary and swore to lay off intoxicating liquors in exchange for a $100 bonus to his salary if he succeeded.

He would part with the same amount if he failed.[42] It was a good thing he did not take the same pledge prior to 1888 because by June he had binged in New York, earning a $100 fine and indefinite suspension from Cincinnati manager Gus Schmelz.[43]

He was not the only Red Stocking to let down his guard in 1888. Schmelz and his owner in the Queen City, Aaron Stern, decided to go a similar route and put drinking clauses into the contracts of all their men prior to the 1889 season. Stern inserted language into the contracts of his players stating that should they falter and intoxicate themselves between the beginning of April and the end of October, they forfeited $500 of their salary back to the team's management. They felt impelled to this extreme step because "this year of '88 the Cincinnati Club suffered through the intemperance—the notorious intemperance—of several members," Baldwin included.[44] The team went 80-54, even with so many players lushing, but still landed in fourth place, eighteen games back of the St. Louis Browns, so it was clear they needed drastic measures to make up the difference. It did not work, however, and the Red Stockings finished fourth again in 1889, eighteen games back once more.

The idea of inserting special "booze contracts" into the regular player contract was a popular one in the American Association. Such were the fears about players and drinking that, by 1887, the National League tried to insert "ironclad" contractual language prescribing heavy penalties towards men who drank while the season was in progress. Before the 1887 season opened, the League amended its constitution to read, "Any person under contract with a League club who shall be guilty of drunkenness, gambling in any form, or any dishonorable or disreputable conduct, may be fined, or may be suspended for the remainder of the season, or for the whole of the ensuing season."[45]

This was straightforward, and the penalty had the potential to be quite severe. Teams ran certain risks in traveling this path, however. The arbitrariness of words like *dishonorable* and *disreputable* left a whole host of behaviors open to interpretation. Then teams faced the question of what to do with players, like Pete Browning, King Kelly, or Jim McCormick, who imbibed often but were excellent players at the same time. Might a team look the other way in their cases but suspend a lesser player to "send a message" about drinking, thus risking accusations of inconsistency? Even if the team was inconsistent, did the team even care? No fan was going to decide to come to the ballpark or stay home based on whether Fatty Briody was the catcher that day, but they might stay away if they knew that Louisville had suspended Pete Browning for drinking, and he was not in the lineup.

In Boston, the Triumvirs decided not to take the chance on appearing inconsistent. During the 1887 season they, like Spalding the year before, employed a detective to shadow their men, and the detective noted not one or two men, but nine, from the club frequenting grog shops in August. The team slapped each man, Sam Wise, Billy Nash, Charlie Radbourn, Con Daily, Dick Johnston, Bill Stemmyer, Tom O'Rourke, Kid Madden, and Bobby Wheelock, with a twenty-five dollar fine for "frequenting disreputable places" and their "infringement of discipline by drinking." This certainly caused dissention in the ranks. Some of the men, such as veteran Sam Wise, admitted they deserved their penalties but found it rather rough that team management came down so hard on youngsters like Billy Nash, who ended up paying $6.25 in fines for each of his four beers.[46] The fines, and the poor morale that resulted from them, may well have caused Boston to falter in the National League standings. The day after the fines came down, the team mauled Pittsburgh by the remarkable score of 28-14, giving it a record of 49-40 for the season. From that point forward, however, the Beaneaters won just twelve times against twenty defeats, turning a moderately promising season into an unremarkable fifth place showing in the National League.

It is a wonder the same detective did not report second baseman Jack Burdock among the delinquent nine, for "Black Jack" certainly could imbibe with the best. He had been in major league baseball since his 1872 debut with the Brooklyn Atlantics, but by 1887, he was merely a part-time player on the Beantown nine. One contemporary referred to him as a man "not especially brilliant when he is sober," and by the winter of 1887, friends reported he "has been drinking hard all winter." After one drinking episode on New Year's Eve of 1887, Burdock barged into a stationary store in Brooklyn near the Washington Park baseball grounds where the Brooklyn club played. He tried to arrest "Tillie Brown, a pretty girl of 17," claiming that he had a warrant for her arrest and that the young woman had to go with him to New York City. Brown, understandably alarmed and terrified, nonetheless kept her composure long enough to ask Burdock to show his warrant and badge, and when he could not do so, said she needed to find her hat and gloves before she could go and asked Burdock to help her find them. As soon as Burdock turned his back, Brown eluded abduction by sprinting out of the store and straight to her sister's house, and in short order, the Brooklyn police issued a warrant for Burdock's arrest on two counts, impersonating an officer and assault.[47]

Despite this, the Boston club signed him for another campaign in 1888 while waiting for the courts to hear the case, hoping to squeeze a bit more value out of the veteran infielder. Burdock's contract was a modest one, offering $1,000 up front and another $1,000 at the season's end pending his good behavior over the summer.[48] Burdock did not come through, however, posting one of the most dismal seasons ever by a player who played semi-regularly or more. Between Boston and Brooklyn that year, he managed to bat .142 in 325 at-bats, for a rock-bottom OPS+ of 11. It was his last season in the major leagues, save for three games in 1891. About the only thing to go right for Black Jack that year was that a judge acquitted him of the charge of assaulting Miss Brown in September when Brown failed to appear in court. According to the *New York Times*, "The court advised Burdock to stop drinking and play ball."[49] He failed to do so, however. By June, he was absent without leave from the Beaneaters: "He says he went as Boston Club delegate to the Brotherhood meeting. President John Ward says he didn't, and the other Boston players know nothing about it. . . . He has not been in condition to play ball, and now it is all over. . . . He may not be officially released this minute, but he will be free to go wherever he wishes within twenty-four hours."[50]

Incredibly, Brooklyn picked Burdock up soon afterward and installed him as its regular second baseman. His offensive performance for the Beaneaters had been less than worthless, but in Brooklyn he played more poorly still, posting a .122 batting average in 259 at-bats in the City of Churches. The team would have been vastly better off by keeping Bill McClellan at second base. McClellan was by no means a strong player but at least managed an OPS+ of 80. Brooklyn's owner, Charles Byrne, decided to take a flyer on Burdock, however, reasoning that with a wife and five children in Brooklyn, Burdock would brace up and play decent ball in his hometown, but it did not happen that way. At least it was a cheap flyer—Burdock allowed Byrne to name the terms of the contract in return for one last opportunity.[51] On the field, the consequence was that Burdock's WAR of -2.0 went almost half-way to costing Brooklyn the pennant in '88. Had the club strengthened itself at second base instead of weakening itself with Burdock, they would have taken the St. Louis Browns all the way to the season's final days, rather than needing ten straight wins just to close the year at six-and-a-half games back. To his credit, Burdock did avoid booze while in Brooklyn, with manager Bill McGunnigle stating, "'Burdie' played poor ball at times, but he never drank a drop from the time he came to us until he was released,"[52] but his performance was so dismal the Bridegrooms let him go at the end of the campaign.[53]

In a story echoing Burdock's, an episode occurred involving Jack O'Connor, a young player with the Cincinnati Reds. One day early in 1888, O'Connor and a few of his friends decided to have some fun with the help of alcohol and ended up behind bars. In a caper that helped earn him his sobriquet of "Rowdy Jack,"

O'Connor and his comrades "wanted to scare a couple of damsels by impersonating police officers and arresting them, and while the boys were playing the joke on the thoroughly scared dusky females they were arrested and locked up for impersonating police officers."[54]

Abusing alcohol also sabotaged the careers of players who should have been major league players but never got there because of their losing battle with demon rum. For instance, whiskey led to the incarceration of Andy Cummins, who got one year in a Kentucky prison for stealing chickens in 1888. One writer described Cummins' talent by stating, "A few years ago Cummins was one of the best all-round base ball players in the country—a hard hitter, sure fielder and a splendid sprinter. Harry Wright once offered him $3,000 a year to play ball and keep sober, but his love for the ardent was too much. He has been arrested several times in the past few years for stealing, but always got off with a workhouse sentence."[55]

At this point, it is worth asking why teams continued giving men second and third chances when they nearly always struck out on such attempts. Someone who had seen one disappointment after another, Albert Mott of Baltimore, once stated, "The best policy for managers to adopt to compel players to abstain from the improper use of liquors is not to employ hard-drinking men. All other plans fail in the end, not only in base ball, but in everything else. Lushing is a disease from which few recover, even among the most intelligent classes."[56] Regardless of whether he was correct, what else could teams do in their seemingly futile search for an entire team of sober, reliable players?

For minor league owners, one option was to locate your team in a town or state that was dry. Minor league clubs might use local drinking regulations to their advantage, like the Portland, Maine, club did when signing Lew Dickerson for 1887. Dickerson was an above-average major league player when sober, posting a career OPS+ of 121, but was not sober nearly often enough. Portland, therefore, thought it might land a useful player by bringing

Dickerson to a town where his vice was not available to him: "There is some chance of keeping Lew straight in the Maine prohibition city, as he can only work his liquor through prescriptions."[57] Portland's plan worked, and Dickerson rehabilitated himself in the eyes of some observers: "What's the matter with Lew Dickerson being given another chance with some League or Association club next season? He has evidently remained perfectly straight all season and has played a splendid second base for Portland, and splendid second basemen are not to be found on every bush."[58] One Philadelphia writer agreed, stating, "Drink has always been his failing, but he is said not to have touched a drop for a year and a half and his reformation appears to be permanent. In view of the great scarcity of competent second basemen, the Phillies might go further and fair worse."[59] Philadelphia did not bite, however, and Dickerson found no other takers, either, never again donning a major league uniform.

Although his flirtation with sobriety gained him some boosters among major league observers, Dickerson signed with London, Ontario, of the International League for the 1888 season, playing shortstop there.[60] He even began the year as team captain, a testament to his skills and the depth of his commitment to a healthier lifestyle. Sad to report, his old habits caught up with him while playing north of the border. In early June, he, along with former major leaguer Larry Corcoran and future major leaguer Tom Kinslow, went on a drinking spree at the Clarence House in London that was so extreme it left Corcoran temporarily paralyzed. Dickerson had to pay a fifty-dollar fine, London fined Corcoran and suspended him without pay, and the club threatened all the men with dismissal from the team and the blacklist should the event repeat itself.[61] As a result, by the winter of 1888-1889 all talk of Dickerson returning to major league baseball died down, one writer dismissing such a possibility by writing, "Lew Dickerson is in town. Dick isn't in the condition he was last winter. He is pretty fat."[62] Things got worse during the 1889 season, alcohol abuse again being the main reason. He spent some time in jail for abusing his wife while drunk, and when he got out, he skipped town and deserted the team, for which the London club suspended him indefinitely.[63]

Another man who swore off intoxicating liquor for the sake of trying to save his career, although temporarily, as it turned out, was William "Peek-A-Boo" Veach. His penchant for drinking prodigious quantities of alcohol was so well-known that once, when a story circulated that other members of his team had quaffed as many beers as he had, a writer refuted such nonsense by observing, "Any one acquainted with Veach knows he can drink enough to drown himself in, and to say that others of the nine drank as much is folly. It has been the bane of his life."[64] Although he played in just a handful of major league games in the 1880s because no one could count on him to be sober, this man was on friendly terms with many of major league baseball's leading drunkards. In an 1887 letter to *The Sporting News*, he described how he was a drinking pal of Billy Taylor, having last seen him in Savannah, and then detailed a bender with Lew Dickerson, Charley Sweeney, and Bill Harbridge in Syracuse back in 1886. Veach described how "we drank so much beer in one saloon that the bar tender sat down and cried like a child." By the end of the night, Veach "kept the bell boy running for bromide of potassium for Harbridge" (medical beliefs of the time considered potassium bromide a useful sedative) while Sweeney "laid perfectly stiff and the only signs of life he gave was that every once in a while he would roll his eyes and say: 'Dear mamma.'" By late 1887, however, Veach had sworn off liquor, which was such a radical departure from his previous habits that some suggested he change his nickname from "Peek-A-Boo" to "Prohibitionist."[65] Still, when he moved from Des Moines, Iowa, and signed to play in St. Paul, Minnesota, for the 1888 season, St. Paul management hedged its bets, offering him a $600 bonus come October should he stay true to his pledge throughout the season.[66] Apparently unable to believe that a man could reform so thoroughly, stories circulated immediately that Veach had gone back on his pledge, so he once again denied them in print. In May he wrote, "I am sure it will be satisfaction to know that I have kept my word."[67]

This story involving Veach is important because in their effort to elevate the moral stature of the game and its players, team executives and the sporting press went out of their way to play up stories suggesting moral reform. They were only too happy to print statements such as those offered by men like Veach and Lefty Marr, a utility player who became a regular performer with the Columbus Solons in 1889. Marr once wrote, "When I first started out as a professional ball player, I thought I could not play ball without I had two or three big drinks of booze. I used to think it gave me courage. I have only found out lately that it was a great detriment. I did not drink a drop all of last season, and I hit the ball better than I ever did."[68] Part of the problem for baseball, however, was that stories of successful reform were rare while stories of reformist players backsliding and returning to being lushing inebriates were common.

While the media did all in its power to play up stories of moral reform, hoping to raise the stature of baseball in the eyes of the public, unfortunately, their shining moral heroes of one day too often became the goats of the next. Veach, for instance, did not keep his word permanently. Playing in California in 1889, "When the Sacramentos lose he drowns his sorrow in the flowing bowl. When they win, he celebrates the victory by getting hilariously full. He did the latter last night, and that is why it reads on the record book this morning: 'Veach—drunk—fined $20 and suspended without pay.'"[69]

Successes did occur occasionally, however. A few players turned themselves around for good, and it happened just often enough to give teams a glimmer of hope that maybe this time a player would come through and become the performer everyone hoped he could be. George Wood was one such man, apparently. When the talented outfielder went from Detroit to the Philadelphia Quakers following the 1885 season, despite the fine .290/.315/.428 batting line he had just put together, the Wolverine faithful displayed little wailing or gnashing of teeth: "Wood is a spasmodic player. There is no doubt he can, when inclined, put as good an article of base ball on the market as one would care to see but while one day his record would glitter with great hits and fine plays, the next (owing to a surplus of conviviality the preceding evening) he would endeavor to bat five or six balls when only one left the pitcher's hand."[70]

Wood later braced up, however. His reputation improved to the extent that, in 1888, Al Spalding invited Wood to travel on his international baseball tour. Given Spalding's fanaticism for sobriety, it is quite unlikely he would have invited Wood if Wood's reputation had not risen a notch or two. The reporters covering the Spalding Tour did not mention him for any heavy drinking, either, even when several other members of the tour started crooking the elbow and earning Spalding's anger, so it seems safe to assume his reformation was complete. The problem for baseball's reputation was that it had many men like Peek-A-Boo Veach and comparatively few like George Wood.

This foray into the role of drinking in 1880s baseball does show that, without doubt, team management had reason to worry about the morals and behavior of their players. The financial stakes for the teams were high. Especially in the National League, where the minimum ticket price was fifty cents, teams hoped to attract wealthier and supposedly respectable patrons to their grounds as the core of their fan base. Such people, however, were not likely to come in the first place, and certainly were not likely to return, if they saw a group of drunken men staggering around the diamond. If teams wanted to encourage these types of people to patronize their games, they had to have men who met the expectations for comportment of middle-class Americans.

Part of the problem, however, was that it was difficult to differentiate fines and disciplinary measures that players truly deserved from those simply meant to keep players fearful for their position and to help ownership recoup their wages. Because everything was arbitrary, with few appeals other than the legal system, where the yawning chasm between the player's resources and ownership's resources led to the same disadvantages that workers faced in the business world generally, efforts at player discipline often resulted in increasing bitterness between players and management. The result of this was, frequently, an adversarial relationship between management and the players, which made contract features such as the reserve clause even more galling because players had no way out of this bad situation, save pleading for release in the hope that another club might prove willing to offer them the chance to play.

Still, it is difficult not to feel some sympathy for team management on this issue. A player such as Mike Kelly might drink constantly, but if that player was talented enough to help the team win despite the drinking, what could a team do? The choice was sell or release the player, or put up with the drinking and take the bad along with the good. In baseball, where the demand for top talent always exceeds the supply, it was exceptionally risky to let a good ballplayer go regardless of his personal habits unless the team had a sure thing as a replacement, and rarely was that the case at a time when teams considered fourteen men a full roster. As a result, teams continued to cast about for solutions as the 1880s progressed, but without lasting success.

---

[1] *Spalding's Official 1889 Base Ball Guide*, (New York: A.G. Spalding & Bros, 1889): 56. While the guide listed no official author, Spalding not wanting to share credit with anyone on the cover of his company's publication, Henry Chadwick was the most important contributor. To clarify nomenclature, in 1880s baseball "kicking" signified complaining or arguing, and the ability to kick effectively was an important attribute for a team captain. Cap Anson, Spalding's captain in Chicago, was legendary at kicking. The word "coaching" translates into trash talking or verbally abusing opposing players. At the time, it had nothing to do with

instructing players like it does today. In fact, the reason that the coaching boxes exist where they do on the field today has nothing to do with where the first or third base coaches used to stand. Instead, their placement reflects the fact that in the 1880s, before the boxes existed, players who were good at coaching would literally stand just a few feet away from opposing batters (or opposing catchers, when their team was at bat) and subject them to a barrage of insults while they tried to perform. St. Louis Browns first baseman and future Chicago White Sox owner Charlie Comiskey was the king of this type of coaching. Eventually, to reduce the abuse to more tolerable levels, baseball owners decided to draw lines on the field for the coachers to stand inside.

[2] "The New Form of Contract," *The Sporting Life*, April 13, 1887, 7.

[3] M. A. T., "From Detroit," *The Sporting Life*, January 13, 1886, 1. M. A. T. was Detroit sportswriter Charles Matheson, sporting editor of the *Detroit Free Press*.

[4] "From Providence," *The Sporting Life*, November 17, 1886, 1. *The Sporting Life* offered that Farrell might have been faltering on purpose to secure his release from the organization because his batting average had declined from .305 in 1883 to .217 in 1884 and .206 in 1885. The paper also reported rumors that Farrell may have been guilty of dissipation. Farrell himself claimed that an attack of rheumatism was the cause of his problems. "News and Notes," *The Sporting Life*, November 17, 1886, 3.

[5] "Diamond Dust," *Chicago Daily Tribune*, August 4, 1886, 3.

[6] W. U. D., "From Washington," *The Sporting Life*, September 14, 1887, 1; W. U. D., "From the Capital," *The Sporting Life*, September 21, 1887, 1.

[7] W. U. D., "From the Capital," *The Sporting Life*, October 12, 1887, 5.

[8] Henry Chadwick, "Chadwick's Chat," *The Sporting Life*, March 28, 1888, 4. Chadwick had, by this time, authored articles on baseball for no less than three encyclopedias: *Chambers' Cyclopedia*, *Appleton's Cyclopedia*, and *Johnson's Cyclopedia*. Some observers jokingly called Barnie the "Bald Eagle of Baltimore" because he was quite bald.

[9] Remlap, "A New Scheme," *The Sporting Life*, August 4, 1886, 1. Remlap was Chicago sportswriter Harry Palmer, who spelled his last name in reverse for a time when signing his articles for *The Sporting Life*.

[10] R. W. L., "On Their Trail," *The Sporting News*, August 9, 1886, 1.

[11] Mugwump, "Hub Happenings," *The Sporting Life*, June 13, 1888, 9.

[12] "No Lushing in the Pittsburg Club," *The Sporting News*, March 30, 1889, 1.

[13] Remlap, "Remlap's Letter," *The Sporting Life*, August 11, 1886, 4.

[14] "Notes and Comments," *The Sporting Life*, August 11, 1886, 5; "Notes and Comments," *The Sporting Life*, August 25, 1886, 5.

[15] "Notes and Comments," *The Sporting Life*, December 1, 1886, 3.

[16] "Notes and Comments," *The Sporting Life*, January 6, 1886, 3.

[17] "Notes and Comments," *The Sporting Life*, January 20, 1886, 3.

[18] "Notes and Comments," *The Sporting Life*, March 3, 1886, 3.

[19] H. E. K., "The White Stockings," *The Sporting News*, March 17, 1886, 1.

[20] "Notes and Comments," *The Sporting Life*, January 26, 1887, 3.

[21] T. T. T., "From Baltimore," *The Sporting Life*, February 2, 1887, 4.

[22] "From the Mound City," *The Sporting Life*, January 6, 1886, 2.

[23] "From Baltimore," *The Sporting Life*, January 6, 1886, 2.

[24] "Notes and Comments," *The Sporting Life*, January 6, 1886, 3.

[25] "Barnie Gets Houck," *The Sporting Life*, February 17, 1886, 1.

[26] "Houck Catches On," *The Sporting Life*, April 13, 1887, 1.

[27] S. A. M., "The Washington Team," *The Sporting News*, August 13, 1887, 5.

[28] T. T. T., "Baltimore Bulletin," *The Sporting Life*, February 8, 1888, 4.

[29] "Caught on the Fly," *The Sporting News*, February 11, 1888, 5.

[30] T. T. T., "Baltimore Bulletin," *The Sporting Life*, February 8, 1888, 4.

[31] T. T. T., "Baltimore Bulletin," *The Sporting Life*, February 15, 1888, 2.

[32] "The Latest News," *The Sporting News*, May 26, 1888, 1.

[33] T. T. T., "Baltimore Bulletin," *The Sporting Life*, February 8, 1888, 4.

[34] Joe Pritchard, "St. Louis Siftings," *The Sporting Life*, March 7, 1888, 2.

[35] "Base-Ball Notes," *Chicago Daily Tribune*, March 22, 1888, 6. The bleaching boards were the uncovered seats at the ballpark, so named, apparently, because during hot summer games the sun bleached the unprotected spectators there.

[36] John Ward, "Ward's Opinion of Denny," *The Sporting Life*, March 7, 1888, 5.

[37] Henry Chadwick, "Chadwick's Chat," *The Sporting Life*, January 26, 1887, 2.

[38] Pritchard, "From St. Louis," *The Sporting Life*, February 2, 1887, 4.

[39] Looker On, "From New York," *The Sporting Life*, February 9, 1887, 1.

[40] Jerry Denny, "A Missive From Denny," *The Sporting Life*, March 2, 1887, 1.

[41] "Affairs at Detroit," *The Sporting News*, August 13, 1887, 2.

[42] "Caught on the Fly," *The Sporting News*, December 11, 1886, 3.

[43] "Notes and Comments," *The Sporting Life*, June 13, 1888, 10.

[44] Ren Mulford, Jr., "Cincinnati Chips," *The Sporting Life*, November 7, 1888, 4.

[45] Henry Chadwick, "Chadwick's Chat," *The Sporting Life*, January 26, 1887, 2.

[46] Mugwump, "From the Hub," *The Sporting Life*, September 7, 1887, 5; "Radbourne Suspended," *The Sporting News*, September 10, 1887, 1.

[47] George Stackhouse, "A Fall from Grace," *The Sporting Life*, January 4, 1888, 1.

[48] Mugwump, "Hub Happenings," *The Sporting Life*, March 14, 1888, 2.

[49] F.O.R., "The League," *The Sporting Life*, March 7, 1888, 1; "Short Stops," *New York Times*, September 2, 1888, 3.

[50] Mugwump, "Changes at Boston," *The Sporting Life*, June 27, 1888, 6.

[51] Ren Mulford, Jr., "Cincinnati Chips," *The Sporting Life*, July 11, 1888, 8.

[52] Mugwump, "Hub Happenings," *The Sporting Life*, November 7, 1888, 6.

[53] "Notes and Comments," *The Sporting Life*, October 24, 1888, 2.

[54] Joe Pritchard, "St. Louis Siftings," *The Sporting Life*, February 29, 1888, 4.

[55] "Notes and Comments," *The Sporting Life*, December 5, 1888, 2.

[56] T. T. T., "From Baltimore," *The Sporting Life*, January 26, 1887, 2.

[57] "Notes and Comments," *The Sporting Life*, April 20, 1887, 11.

[58] "Caught on the Fly," *The Sporting News*, October 22, 1887, 4.

[59] "Philadelphia Pointers," *The Sporting Life*, November 16, 1887, 2.

[60] "Gossip from Cincinnati," *The Sporting Life*, December 28, 1887, 1; "Notes and Comments," *The Sporting Life*, December 28, 1887, 5.

[61] "The Latest News," *The Sporting News*, June 9, 1888, 1.

[62] Circle, "Pittsburg Pencilings," *The Sporting Life*, January 16, 1889, 3.

[63] "Notes and Comments," *The Sporting Life*, July 10, 1889, 4.

[64] Prowler, "The Des Moines Poet," *The Sporting News*, February 11, 1888, 3.

[65] Peek-A-Boo, the Prohibitionist, "Peek-A-Boo Veach," *The Sporting News*, December 31, 1887, 1.

[66] "How a Pitcher Signed," *The Sporting Life*, January 11, 1888, 1.

[67] Peekaboo Veach, the Prohibitionist, "Peekaboo Veach," *The Sporting News*, May 19, 1888, 1.

[68] "Notes and Comments," *The Sporting Life*, November 21, 1888, 6.

[69] "Veach Again Suspended," *The Sporting News*, July 27, 1889, 1.

[70] M. A. T., "From the City of the Straits" *The Sporting Life*, December 16, 1885, 1.

Chapter 3

Beliefs About Player Fitness

In addition to avoiding problems with alcohol, baseball teams believed physical training and the condition of the players throughout the season was crucial to success in Gilded Age baseball. True, in the 1880s there were no personal trainers, nutritional supplements (legal or otherwise), or advanced weightlifting regimens, and the concept of going to spring training to prepare for a new season was in its infancy. This does not mean, however, that players simply showed up at the ballpark on opening day to play ball after sitting around for five or six months. Instead, most of them participated in various kinds of off-season workout routines to make sure they stayed sharp and ready for their next campaign.

Just like with alcohol, however, part of the reason teams cared about player conditioning was financial. In fact, this was probably the most important reason that team managers took measures to keep their nine in shape over the winter. It was true, of course, that teams with many players who were fat and out of shape would not perform as well on the field. Baseball players were athletes, and like in most sports, having men who were fast, strong, and possessed endurance was an advantage. They were also an advantage at the ticket window.

The prevailing belief among almost all observers of the game was that fans came to the grounds to see action. They wanted to see batters hit the ball, fielders chase it, and baserunners on the move. Fans disliked lengthy games with long waits for batters to swing, little action for the fielders, timid baserunning, or lackadaisical effort by the men in the field. They would not, in other words, care much for baseball today, when games take three hours or more and some players put the ball in play only half the time they come to bat. This is not to say that all games had to have lots of runs to please the cranks, however. On the contrary, newspapers often reported low-scoring games as among the best of the year because low-scoring games generally meant the fielders had performed well and made exciting plays. Although fans wanted their team to win, of course, the level of scoring was not the critical consideration—the amount of action that fans witnessed was what people cared about most. When commentators stated that fans wanted "heavy batting," they did not necessarily mean people expected a continual parade of long hits; instead, they meant that fans wanted to see lots of contact with the ball and movement in the field.

As a result, whenever the legislators of the game tinkered with the rules, they did so hoping to create more action. Strikeouts, although considered among the most important stats for a pitcher to accumulate today, were not very popular to fans or managers in the 1880s. This was partly because commentators favored "headwork" from pitchers with a scientific approach to their craft but also because when the batter struck out, nothing happened in the field. The same was true of baserunners who were not a threat to steal after reaching base. They put no pressure on the defense and thus created no excitement for spectators.

This meant that teams put a high value on men who could create excitement in the field. That is what fans paid to see, and that is what teams tried to give them. Players with great speed were always in demand; in fact, sometimes, wealthy supporters of the teams offered prizes to the men who stole the most bases during a season. The same was true of those with great defensive range who could track down balls in the field and prevent hits. When newspapers described the attributes of a player, they generally discussed the man's batting skill, defensive ability, and baserunning reputation, without indicating that they regarded any of these categories as more important than the others. Sometimes, managers declared their intent to have a "baserunning team," indicating that many believed emphasizing swift men on the base paths was a legitimate strategy to achieve victory.

For example, when asked about his nine's chances in 1886, Louisville manager Jim Hart stated, "In base-running, which counts a great deal, the club is very superior, while in general playing ability we have none to fear. Our men are all young, full of life and activity, and will surpass in every instance their individual records of last year."[1] Later, Hart added, "Make a note of this: the club is strong at batting, strong in its batteries, and strong in base running, just where we were lacking last season. What better prospect do we want?"[2] Likewise, when Al Spalding's Chicago team finished its spring training stint in Hot Springs, Arkansas, in 1886, he described the players' fitness for action in 1886 by stating, "In battery and batting strength, in infielding and outfielding, in base running and base stealing and in every point of play that goes to make up a crack team, our boys showed in thoroughly satisfactory form last season as I believe they will this."[3]

Because of these beliefs, the level of physical fitness of the nine was always an important consideration for managers and owners. Players must stay in good shape, or be "in the pink of condition," so they could perform up to the expectations of the spectators. Men who were "ice wagons" might cost their clubs money if the cranks believed they were paying for inferior baseball played by flabby, out-of-shape athletes.[4] As a result, teams did many things to encourage their men to be in top condition because ticket receipts depended on it. Similar to the alcohol issue, a well-conditioned nine would win more games, and that helped draw fans, but for management an equally real fear was that, win or lose, fans would refuse to come to the park to see players who could not keep up with the opposition athletically.

Fans and sportswriters, apparently, worried about this issue as well. When the Chicago White Stockings went to the very first spring training in Hot Springs, Arkansas in 1886, they brought along team sportswriter Harry Palmer to report their progress to the sporting public. Palmer responded by supplying readers with a before-and-after table of player weights so that fans would know how their favorite man was getting into form. However, Palmer did not stop there. His readers also learned the exact physical measurements of each White Stocking player. Team captain Anson, for instance, sported a 41.75-inch chest, 14.75-inch biceps, 14.75-inch forearms, 26-inch thighs, 16.75-inch calves, and stood six-foot-two. Ace pitcher John Clarkson, in comparison, measured a scrawny 37.25, 13, 12.75, 23, 14.25, and five-foot-nine, respectively.[5] Not wanting to let the White Stockings outdo them, the Boston Beaneaters followed the same procedure of letting their fans know the size and conditioning of various members of their nine in 1886. Their correspondent for *The Sporting Life* reported that "Burdock is the most evenly and best developed man of the team. . . . Stemmyer is the tallest man . . . and the heaviest. . . . He has also the greatest lung capacity, 340 cubic inches, and the largest hip. Wise has the largest calf. . . . The youngest player is Nash, and the lightest is Poorman, 135 pounds."[6]

Part of the attraction of going to Hot Springs was that people believed that hot springs had important medicinal qualities that would aid players trying to get into top form. Chicago shortstop Ned Williamson put it well when, after a ride to nearby Sulphur Springs, he wrote back to his hometown *Chicago Daily Tribune* "The curative properties of the waters here are really wonderful, as demonstrated in several cases of rheumatism. Last Wednesday a big fellow weighing close upon 200 pounds arrived here, and was apparently so lame that he could hardly walk with the aid of crutches, and Saturday he won a hundred-yard race from Anson; result, Anson $50 loser."[7] Williamson closed his letter by writing, "The boys are all looking splendid. The baths weaken us some, but when we get through with them we shall settle right down to hard work and put in about five hours a day in the field with the bat and ball. When we do go North again—well, just keep your eye on the champions."[8]

The idea of using water to cure various ailments was not new in the 1880s. A handful of physicians, both American and European, promoted it in association with other restorative activities as the best way to regain health. One of its most famous proponents was Vincent Priessnitz, who practiced in what was then Austrian Silesia (Czech Republic today) during the 1840s. Some of his apostles, notably Thomas Nichols, Joel Shew, and R.T. Trall, brought Priessnitz's techniques to the United States in 1843, when they opened an establishment in New York City and started publishing the *Water-Cure Journal*, which had a print run lasting from 1844 to 1913. Uses of water in healing included general bathing, various types of showers, plunging into the water, dripping water on an ailment, and soaking sheets or blankets and applying them to unhealthy areas of the body. The cures these people promoted had many things in common in addition to water, however. Water healers also advised their patients to escape from unhealthy and stressful city living, diet to eliminate excess eating, exercise frequently, live in a communal setting promoting recovery, and let nature take its course. Considering how dirty, unsanitary, and crowded American cities were in the mid-19th century, this was probably sound advice in many cases.[9]

Still practicing into the 1870s, Trall even co-authored a book advising patients to combine water and proper diet to remedy illness. He also told his readers they should abstain from using alcohol or tobacco. By 1894, a German immigrant named Benedict Lust was a major figure in American hydropathy, building on the efforts of a fellow German, Father Sebastian Kneipp, and by 1896, he was advising patients in his New York City practice to employ water, light, chiropractors, a quality diet, exercise, baths, and massage to improve their lives. Both future United States president Theodore Roosevelt and the ill-fated Austrian Archduke Franz Ferdinand endorsed these methods.[10] Considering that the idea of hydropathy enjoyed some general popularity and intellectual respectability, it was, therefore, no great leap of faith for the White Stockings to head to Hot Springs and hope for some medicinal benefit from the waters there. We should probably note that people today generally agree with this assessment of the value of hot water, if the number of hot tubs dotting backyards throughout the world is any indication of people's confidence in the restorative value of water.

Spalding believed that the waters at Hot Springs had other favorable traits as well. Before departing, he discussed his plan with a writer from *The Sporting News*, saying, "It's a great scheme, I wonder whatever made me think of it. All the boys are enthusiastic about it and all want to go. . . . I boil out all the alcoholic microbes which may have impregnated the systems of these men during the winter while they have been away from me and Anson. Once get the microbes out, and the danger of a relapse is slight."[11] Limiting alcohol, as we know well, was never far from Spalding's mind.

Another interesting aspect of the views most observers held about player fitness was the importance placed on simple size. By the mid-1880s, all conceded that the Detroit Wolverines had the most impressive roster of physical specimens ever assembled: "The Detroits are the biggest set of men ever gathered into one team, Manning being the only medium-sized man in the team. In Brouthers, White, Thompson and Twitchell the team has giants, while Rowe, Richardson, Hanlon, and Bennett are very large, heavy men. . . . Wherever they go the Detroits evoke praise for their fine physical appearance."[12]

To provide perspective on who people considered a large man in the Gilded Age, Dan Brouthers stood 6' 2", 207 pounds, and Sam Thompson the same. Deacon White was 5'11", 175, although being 38 years old by this time, he may well have been heavier than the official tally. One writer stated, "Jim White may be getting old, but if he is as frisky on the ball field, as he is at the table he improves with age."[13] Larry Twitchell measured 6', 185, while Jack Rowe was 5'8", 170 pounds, Hardy Richardson 5' 9", 170, equal to Ned Hanlon, and Charlie Bennett was 5'11", 180. Jim Manning, the "medium" man, stood 5'7" and weighed 157 pounds. For comparison, the tallest player in the American Association was John Reilly who, like Brouthers and Thompson, stood 6'2".

Reflecting this obsession with size, Detroit's cranks even knew the waist sizes of their ballplayers in 1887. For example, catcher Charlie Bennett featured a waist of thirty-five inches. True to his nickname, "Big" Sam Thompson required a 36.5-inch belt, while "Big" Dan Brouthers sported a waistline of thirty-eight inches, the greatest girth on the team. In comparison, twenty-year-old pitcher Pete Conway was a mere twig, featuring a 32.75-inch waist.[14]

The modern reader might find these numbers interesting, considering that men of the stature of Brouthers or Thompson would be respectable, but hardly remarkable, in baseball today, while fans would consider Manning a runt. Both Brouthers and Thompson had the nickname "Big," so we can assume they truly stood out from contemporaries. The reason for the difference, of course, is that over the past century the average person's diet has improved remarkably. Despite the health problems associated with processed foods, the quantity of food is much greater and more reliable today than it was to many people in the 1880s. Although working-class people in the 1880s worked many hours each week, often more than sixty, their pay was low because so much of the work was unskilled or semi-skilled labor. They could not always afford an adequate, balanced diet, nor were the fruits and vegetables required for a balanced diet always available all seasons of the year like they are today, even for people who could afford them. Exacerbating the problem was the fact that refrigerated rail transportation was a very recent invention, which meant that getting fresh fruit or vegetables out of season was a challenge for anyone, no matter how much money they might have.

The size and weight of the average baseball player reflected these facts. Most baseball fans know that home runs were comparatively rare before 1920—we call the years preceding 1920 the "Deadball Era" to reflect this fact. It is true that the ball lacked some of the spring it has now and that ballparks were larger in those years than they are today, making home runs more difficult to come by. What most fail to remember, however, is that another reason home runs were unusual is that most of the players just were not big enough or strong enough to hit the ball over the fence very often.

When the American Association's Baltimore Orioles reported for training in 1887, they looked to take after their National League brethren from the City of the Straits and find large, strapping men of impressive physical stature. Success crowned their efforts, with one writer reporting "all the members of the Baltimore team are remarkably-built men, and not a man measures less than thirty-seven inches across the chest." The measurements of Baltimore's nine went from young Phenomenal Smith's 38 inches to the Redwood-like 42.75-inch trunk of James "Jumbo" Davis.[15] Davis had a reported playing height and weight of 5'11", 195 pounds, which made him a large man indeed in 1887. Jumbo, "our friend of the large pedal extremities," also earned a reputation for a reluctance to slide into bases because during practice for the 1887 season he belly-flopped into one slide such that he "drove the canvas so far into the soil that you couldn't see it with a telescope."[16]

That same year, the *Cleveland Plain Dealer* gave its nine the rather lukewarm endorsement that the Blues had more uniformity in size than any other team in the American Association. However, it did remember to give a little praise to the players' conditioning, stating that they were "a pretty stalwart and muscular lot of men" who were about to play some of the best ball of their lives.[17] In 1888 the team showed improvement in this regard because some of its new blood were large players: "Nine of them . . . are above the ordinary size, and . . . four are giants." The men who opened the season with the team averaged 5-foot, 7-inches in height and weighed an average of 171 pounds.[18]

Similarly, Louisville looked to beef up its nine for 1887 and find men in the prime of their careers to do battle with the American Association that year. Of the sixteen men in the organization in mid-April, none were older than twenty-nine, and all but four were twenty-six or younger. While it boasted no 200-pounders such as Dan Brouthers or Sam Thompson, the club did have an average weight of 167 pounds, earning the remark that "this is not a Jumbo team, but it is by no means a lightweight aggregation of players."[19]

Although writers and fans praised men for their size, most remembered that baseball is also a game of skill. It was important to differentiate, therefore, between mere size or weight as compared to finding men in the pink of condition, as sportswriters phrased it in the Gilded Age. As the commentary regarding Brouthers, Davis, and others show, being big was only useful if it produced on-field benefits and corresponded to performance. Mere fat drew scorn from commentators. Things got so bad for the Brooklyn Grays in September of 1887, for instance, that the players took heat for carrying too much reserve adipose tissue and the sporting press began referring to them as "ice wagons." George Stackhouse describe Brooklyn's lack of conditioning by writing, "The prodigal son has returned to Brooklyn, but he will not chew juicy steaks cut from the traditional fatted calf. In fact the Brooklyn Club is not killing fatted calves for its players at present. It will plane down some of the extra and flabby tissue on its players first. People around Gotham think that the Brooklyn Club would play better ball if the men were not so fat."[20]

This focus on overweight players and conditioning was especially important to observers, given the value that 1880s baseball's conventional wisdom placed on speed, fielding range, and baserunning skill. George Stackhouse spoke for many, therefore, when he wrote, "It seems a pity that such a ball town as Brooklyn undisputedly is should have such a slow-moving team. Moly Hoses, how slow they are."[21] A prime offender was reserve outfielder Ernie Burch. Described as "one of the largest men in the profession," one of Burch's teammates in Brooklyn described the flabby left fielder by saying, "See that man sitting over there watching the clock? Well, that man is none other than Burch, our left fielder. He will sit in that chair until dinner-time and he will keep one eye on the clock the whole time. He may get up and move around a little, but the chances are that he will not. He is lazy and the biggest feeder on the team."[22]

While Burch stood five-foot ten and weighed 190 pounds, larger still was an outfielder who played in New York named Mike Slattery. Truly a large man during the late-nineteenth century, he measured six-foot two and 210 pounds. Like Burch, Slattery could not convince New York sportswriters that his eating habits always served him well: "I hear that since Esterbrook ceased to be a Giant Slattery has taken his place as the champion feeder of the team. The New York players have frequently remarked that Slattery is nearly always left at the plate when the rest of the team leave the dining room. In this city where Slattery is well known his entrance into a restaurant generally creates a stampede among the waiters."[23]

Might the ridicule heaped on overweight players go in the other direction as well? Did the press also poke fun at lightweight players? Not as often, as it turns out. Players who were not just thin, but truly skinny, might earn notice for this fact, although without the excessively negative connotations that went with being overweight. Dave Foutz, nicknamed "Scissors," was one such player. The nickname itself referenced his appearance when pitching the ball, and one writer referred to Foutz as "his slivership," but despite his scrawny appearance, he was successful as both a hitter and a pitcher up until age started to take its toll in his mid-thirties.[24] Another example was Davy Force, a shortstop with a respectable career lasting from 1871 to 1886. Despite his misleading last name, Force hit just one home run for his entire career, and at five-foot, four-inches and 140 pounds probably never scared anyone. Observers called him "Wee Davy" or "Tom Thumb," but he had a sixteen-year career in baseball all the same, so it is clear he held a measure of respect despite his diminutive stature.

The fascination with player fitness and size even contributed to one of the early spoofs in baseball history. Long before *Sports Illustrated* introduced the world to Sidd Finch in 1985, baseball fans learned of Tsang Wong Foo. On May 15, 1887, with Al Spalding's Chicago club struggling to field a reliable pitching staff outside of leading hurler John Clarkson, the *Milwaukee Sentinel* ran a special dispatch describing Chicago's acquisition of a new pitcher from China who stood six-foot, seven-inches, writing, "This collection of bones, muscle, and gristle was none other than Tsang Wong Foo, an athletic coolie from the village of Kwachu, in the province of Kiangtsu, and he is now a skilled baseball pitcher." The dispatch described how Tsang Wong Foo became a baseball prodigy:

A Chinese professor, after some research, discovered that the art of curving a ball in the air was known during the time of Confucius, and that it was merely a primitive form of the art which had been causing tops to travel up hill in China for the last 1,600 years. Aided by these discoveries the professor at once put twenty men into practice at curving the ball according to the regulations of the National Baseball League. The men soon attained wonderful proficiency. After three months of steady practice Tsang Wong Foo was picked out as the best of the lot and at once placed on the market and shipped to Chicago.[25]

Not only could Tsang Wong Foo curve a ball around posts to strike a nail into an oak plank, he could do so almost as effectively with his left arm as with his right. Furthermore, he once pitched fourteen consecutive hours without resting. In the United States,

Tsang Wong Foo would pitch under the name Mike Murphy, according to the article. Unsurprisingly, no one named Mike Murphy, or Tsang Wong Foo, for that matter, appeared on a major league diamond in 1887, but this faked account does demonstrate the connection many baseball observers made between physical stature, proper training, and athletic prowess.[26]

Spoofs aside, some baseball observers tried to apply athletic science, or what passed for athletic science in the 1880s, to training techniques. The premier manual of training and injury treatment in 1880s baseball was by Dr. Alexander Leuf, titled *Hygiene for Base Ball Players: Being a Brief Consideration of the Body as a Mechanism; the Art and Science of Curve Pitching; a Discussion of the Causes and Treatment of the Disabilities of Players; With a Few Practical Hints to Club Managers*. This book, published in 1888, contained descriptions and diagrams of all manner of motions and training techniques associated with the game. Unlike many contemporaries, however, the author was no quack. Leuf was an M.D., was the director of physical education at the University of Pennsylvania and Swarthmore College at the time he published his book, was an honorary member and the ex-secretary of the Brooklyn Pathological Society, and had worked at St. Mary's hospital in Brooklyn. In addition, some sporting papers quoted him and his research in their columns, so people in baseball recognized his name and put stock in his views on training.

When it came to beliefs about the best way to deal with baseball injuries, Leuf offered several suggestions for treatment. Leuf advised treating the arms of pitchers in various ways. Liniments were inappropriate for treating sore muscles because "in the first place, they are utterly useless, as any number of impartial and disgusted sufferers can testify." Likewise, players should avoid rubbings, massages, or any other passive motion activity to treat soreness because these served no beneficial purpose, either. Leuf advised elevating the arm, believing that the excess blood producing the pressure on the muscle would recede due to gravity, thus

83

relieving the soreness. The player might alternate this with immersion in hot water.[27]

For general muscle injuries, hot water was, by far, the best treatment in Leuf's eyes. A player might combine hot water with plaster bandages and continue to play. Mild galvanism (treatment with electricity) could help as well. Leuf recognized that ballplayers tended to heal from soreness and mild injuries more quickly than the population at large and credited this to better nutrition, which may well have been true. These treatments only worked for muscles, of course. Broken bones and issues that were more serious could only heal with time.[28]

More severe pains called for more active measures: "In severer cases, where there is an excess of inflammatory products, the best remedy is mild galvanism." The timing of the application of electricity was important, too, because "Mild galvanism is very gratifying and should be done in the evening, so that the nutritive changes induced by the passage of the current shall act undisturbed till the next morning." It was important that only experts performed this procedure, however, with Leuf stating, "It is well, however, to bear in mind that very great harm can be done with electricity if not judiciously employed. This can only be done by skilled physicians. No ball player or advertising 'electrician' can do any good for they can never be certain as to the kind of electricity to be used, its quantity and intensity, as well as the duration of its application." This last warning was necessary because some players carried their own batteries with them for treatment while traveling to road games.[29]

Leuf's book also offered advice on how to train and avoid injury in the first place. He advised constant muscular exercise throughout the playing season, the equivalent of what we would call weightlifting. Doctor Leuf also realized that not all baseball activities used the same muscle groups, and so recommended different training regimens depending on the position played. He put great stock in exercise machinery, especially one manufactured by the company of former baseball player Al Reach. This machine, featuring weights manipulated via pulleys and a handle for the player to grip, was a simplified version of today's Universal Gym or Bowflex apparatus. Reach's machine cost ten dollars and came with an illustrated pamphlet demonstrating thirty-one different exercises. Leuf's book illustrated the various exercise movements as well and mentioned what muscles each activity emphasized, sometimes including how performing a certain exercise would aid the ballplayer. The machine even had an attachment so that the player could hook up a bat and practice swinging against mild resistance.[30]

In addition to the Reach exercise machine, Leuf advocated a few more activities. He favored flexibility and endurance over power, cautioning readers that exercise should be slow and that it was best to stop before great fatigue set in. He approved of training with Indian war clubs but cautioned that they should be light and swung slowly. Work with dumbbells was acceptable, but, again, Doctor Leuf advised light weights for exercises where the elbow remained stiff. Besides weights, Leuf agreed with those who preached hand ball as a premier form of exercise: "This will reduce the amount of fat to a minimum within two or three weeks, besides hardening the muscles and getting one fully past the period of soreness and stiffness.[31]

The book closed with general advice on other aspects of staying in top form during the season, some quite sensible, others more dubious. When addressing the question of whether the gymnasium or outside practice was preferable, Leuf wrote, "Gymnasium work in the winter has its use, but proper base ball practice is far better and makes the former not only unnecessary but undesirable." He also advised, for example, practicing twice a day even on game days, although only for thirty minutes for pitchers and catchers, while eating at precisely 7 a.m. for breakfast and 12 noon for lunch. The book discouraged play in cool temperatures, due to the greater risk of injury. It concluded with sections on how to achieve proper digestion (players should not eat before active work, must chew food carefully, and should not eat fried or greasy foods), an admonition to get adequate amounts of sleep, and a warning regarding the importance of abstaining from alcohol and smoking.[32]

Baseball teams of the Gilded Age were surprisingly modern in that they placed great value on physical training and athleticism. The techniques used in achieving this status might not be what a twenty-first century athletic trainer would choose, but the goal was the same. Teams wanted men at a high level of physical ability and preparedness before beginning each season and took significant measures to help their players reach this goal.

A key difference, as we have seen, is in the thinking of why this was necessary. In the present day, where many players train year-round, have nutritionists, lift weights consistently, and take steroids and other drugs, the goal is to keep these finely tuned athletes on the field. A team needs its star players on the field to compete and win, and teams that win draw fans, television money, and the extra revenue associated with playoff appearances. Muscular players with home run power are also good drawing cards, and baseball's powers that be like to see the home runs flying and the scoreboards lit up. Anyone who has watched the game since the early 1990s knows this well. If they do not see enough hits flying over the fence, baseball owners simply instruct the company that manufactures the baseballs to wind the ball tighter, so it will fly farther, or move the fences of their ballparks a few feet closer to home plate. The game today, unlike that of the 1880s, is not a game of motion. Pitchers and their pitching coaches now prize the ability to strike out batters while the better hitting coaches laud their players for their patience in taking pitches and working the pitcher for walks if they can. Batters put the ball in play for the fielders to handle less frequently in the 2010s than they ever have before. Some do so only about half the time they come to bat.

Neither of these things, pitchers attempting to pile up strikeouts or batters trying to draw walks by waiting out the pitcher, were popular in 1880s baseball. Writers often referred to batters who did take a lot of pitches as waiters. Observers did not exactly look down on the strategy, but for most players, taking pitches was more a means to an end, that of getting a good pitch the player thought he could hit hard. In the same vein, when the owners discussed rule changes each year, the goal was to see more hitting and more action. This required athletic men who could both hit the ball hard when at bat and chase and field it proficiently when on defense, and who hopefully could run the bases with vigor as well. Fans wanted to see action, and action helped draw the fans to the park. For a team to draw well, having players meeting all these specifications was almost a requirement. Thus, teams spent much money and energy looking for the best ways to keep their players in prime condition throughout the year, and did so to keep their finances healthy throughout the year.

---

[1] "The Falls City," *The Sporting News*, March 17, 1886, 3.
[2] Ibid. The battery was the combination of pitcher and catcher. Because of the great stress and threat of injury for catchers in these years when gloves and other protective gear were very primitive, some teams assigned an individual catcher to each of its three main pitchers.
[3] Remlap, "Remlap's Letter," *The Sporting Life*, April 7, 1886, 5.
[4] The term "ice wagon" reflected the fact that, before modern refrigeration, people needed to use big blocks of ice if they wanted food to stay cool and last. Because ice is heavy, the wagons that brought ice to people could not move very quickly.
[5] Remlap, "Remlap's Letter," *The Sporting Life*, April 14, 1886, 5.
[6] "Notes and Comments," *The Sporting Life*, April 14, 1886, 5.
[7] "The Sporting World," *Chicago Daily Tribune*, March 27, 1886, 9.
[8] Ibid.
[9] Susan Cayleff, *Nature's Path: A History of Naturopathic Healing in America*, (Baltimore: Johns Hopkins, 2016): 25-27.
[10] Ibid., 14, 27-28.

[11] "The Chicago Team in Hot Water," *The Sporting News*, March 17, 1886, 2. Although this quote fits with the way many Gilded Age people viewed the curative properties of water, Spalding might have meant it as a joke. His next comment was, "If that don't work I'll send 'em all over to Paris next year and have 'em inoculated by Pasteur." Spalding was, however, a strong believer that athletes should abstain from drinking, and Anson thought the same.

[12] "Notes and Comments," *The Sporting Life*, April 21, 1886, 5.

[13] Atlanta, "Dunlap at Atlanta," *The Sporting News*, April 23, 1887, 4.

[14] M. A. T., "Detroit Dotlets," *The Sporting Life*, February 16, 1887, 5.

[15] "Notes and Comments," *The Sporting Life*, April 6, 1887, 5.

[16] T. T. T., "From Baltimore," *The Sporting Life*, April 6, 1887, 6.

[17] "Notes and Comments," *The Sporting Life*, April 6, 1887, 5.

[18] F. H. Brunell, "Brunell's Budget," *The Sporting Life*, April 11, 1888, 4.

[19] X. X. X., "From the Falls City," *The Sporting Life*, April 13, 1887, 7.

[20] George Stackhouse, "New York Mention," *The Sporting Life*, September 21, 1887, 1.

[21] George Stackhouse, "New York Mention," *The Sporting Life*, September 21, 1887, 1.

[22] Joe Pritchard, "St. Louis Siftings," *The Sporting Life*, February 29, 1888, 4.

[23] George Stackhouse, "New York News," *The Sporting Life*, July 18, 1888, 1.

[24] T. T. T., "Baltimore Bulletin," *The Sporting Life*, March 7, 1888, 4.

[25] "A Baseball Giant," *Milwaukee Sentinel*, May 16, 1887, 2.

[26] Ibid.

[27] Alexander Leuf, *Hygiene for Base Ball Players: Being a Brief Consideration of the Body as a Mechanism; the Art and Science of Curve Pitching; a Discussion of the Causes and Treatment of the Disabilities of Players; With a Few Practical Hints to Club Managers*, (Philadelphia: A.J. Reach & Company, 1888): 57.

[28] Ibid., 60.
[29] Ibid., 58-59.
[30] Ibid., 63-95.
[31] Ibid., 95.
[32] Ibid., 95-121.

Chapter 4

Methods of Keeping Fit

Because baseball observers believed being healthy and in good shape to play ball was a prime requisite for ballplayers, it is worth taking the time to explore how the players tried to get in shape and stay there. Unlike drinking alcohol, which was a common pastime throughout the country, exercising for fitness was not a common thing to do in Gilded Age America. Working a job in an industrial factory or operating a farm was plenty of work by itself; most people did not need to do anything extra after work to fight the flab, especially given the limitations on nutrition noted in the last chapter. Places to exercise, known as gymnasiums, existed, but they were much smaller than what that word generally signifies today, and the idea of creating a fitness club with aisles of sophisticated equipment was decades away. Recreational sports had some following, to be sure. Handball was popular for baseball players, and a brief craze for the toboggan swept the Northern states in the 1880s, but other sports that people today often play for exercise, such as basketball, did not exist yet. Even bicycles were relatively new in the 1880s and, while sporting enthusiasts considered cycling a legitimate sport, the idea of making both wheels the same size had not been around long. Some people called this new style of bicycle the "safety bicycle" because it was such a dramatic improvement over previous types in terms of balance and handling.

All this meant that if players wanted to stay in top form, they had to find ways to do so that were not all that common for the general population. Modern medicine was not much help, either. Plenty of companies peddled quack medicines that promised to cure all kinds of ills, but modern contrivances such as protein shakes and steroids did not exist. Some men posed as athletic trainers, but as with medicine, some were legitimate and others not, and sometimes the line between the two was blurry.

Still, teams needed fit, athletic men to play ball. The results on the field and the results at the ticket window demanded it. As a result, even before opening day, teams looked for training schemes and expended money to get their nines ready to play ball. Players did a variety of things in the off-season, some more conducive to successful ball playing than others. Most returned to their home cities for the winter. Others would participate in exhibition tours through the Southern states, California, or even more exotic locales such as the Spanish colony of Cuba, where warmer winter weather allowed them to continue playing and stay in shape for the next season. Come March, some teams would embark for southerly climes as a group, such as the Chicago White Stockings, who made an annual pilgrimage to Hot Springs, Arkansas, in the late 1880s to work into shape. This is the first known instance of what we now call spring training.

It was never too early for teams to tout the fitness of their players to bolster their support with the cranks, either. When the White Stockings went to Arkansas, they brought along team sportswriter Harry Palmer so that he could report back on the men's dramatic progress. He wrote, "Several of them, notably Flint, Williamson, Burns, and Dalrymple will have to drop a few pounds before they can get around the bases in their old-time form, but the majority are all solid bone and muscle and ready to play the best ball of their lives." Palmer went on to supply his readers with a before-and-after table of player weights. Displaying progress that would make good TV advertising for a modern diet plan, shortstop Ned Williamson, pitcher Jim McCormick, and first baseman Cap Anson dropped eight pounds apiece in just two weeks of training, while outfielder George Gore and catcher/outfielder Mike Kelly sloughed off five each. Regarding the health and conditioning of the White Stockings, Williamson reported that the players ran between three and eight miles daily, with the result that "all of the big fellows are rapidly reducing, and the 'lightweights' are gaining in flesh."[1]

Williamson certainly numbered among the "big fellows" attempting to reduce his store of reserve adipose at Hot Springs in 1886. In earlier years, his athletic abilities had been first-class. In 1882, when the White Stockings held contests for the top baserunning speed and distance throwing among their players, Williamson won both, circling the bases in 14.75 seconds and heaving the ball 396 feet on the fly.[2] Things had changed by 1886, however. Having a less-than-svelte playing height and weight of 5'11", 215 pounds, by the time the White Stockings reached Hot Springs, Williamson tipped the scales nearer to 270. An astounded Cap Anson accused Williamson of "having accumulated in the neighborhood of sixty pounds of superfluous adipose during the winter months."[3] Although he dropped a few of those extra pounds while at Hot Springs, his 1886 season was horrible, with Williamson hitting for a pathetic .216 batting average and claiming only 13 stolen bases.

For 1887, then, Williamson tried a preemptive approach to getting in shape. Stopping in at White Stockings headquarters before embarking for the Hot Springs, he astounded all present with his chiseled physique. As Harry Palmer put it, with a heavy dose of stereotyping, "When he left here last fall he was almost Falstaffian in appearance, with a paunch like an alderman, a face like a Dutch brewer, and a heavy, swinging gait like any other than that of an athlete." By early March of 1887, however, Williamson was eager to show off his makeover. After he "swelled his biceps and stuck out one iron-muscled leg for examination," Palmer pronounced the new, 197-pound shortstop "one of the biggest, squarest, whitest men that ever picked a ball off the diamond."[4]

The extra physical preparation certainly helped Williamson. His slash line improved from .216/.339/.335 to .267/.377/.437, his OPS+ rose from 95 to 114, and he hit more doubles, triples, and home runs than he had in 1886 in a comparable number of at bats. Most tellingly, perhaps, his total of stolen bases rose from 13 to 45. Besides his new training regimen, observers also credited his refusal of strong drink for the improvement, one writing "Ned Williamson hasn't touched a drop all this season and has become an enthusiastic advocate and supporter of Spalding's temperance theory. . . . Ned has also made many new and firm friends of a better class than he ever had in the old days, when he thought of nothing but having a good time."[5]

With Williamson now in prime condition, someone else training at Hot Springs (joining the White Stockings were a handful of players employed by other clubs) had to take the ribbing for his resemblance to a Chaucerian friar. That man turned out to be Bill Phillips, Brooklyn's first baseman: "The proud title of alderman should be transferred from him [Williamson] to Old Bill Phillips. Bill's companions have nick-named him Budweiser, which is not exactly to his liking."[6]

The White Stockings pioneered the idea of spring training, but in the 1880s, it was not yet a general practice. Most teams had no mandatory preparatory plans. That meant that players who wanted to be in top form had to do something on their own. As mentioned earlier, some traveled to the South, to Cuba, or to California to work their way into form, but not everyone could do so. For one thing, someone had to organize the tour, which only happened when the organizer believed he might profit, and too many touring teams in the same region at the same time saturated the market for exhibition games. As a result, most players participated in private workout sessions in their home cities. They called their training haunts gymnasiums. Usually these were indoor, an obvious advantage for players wintering in cities such as Chicago or Boston. The practice of renting a gymnasium for practice was already an old one by the mid-1880s. According to a memorandum in the possession of Harry Wright, a member of the legendary Cincinnati Red Stockings team of 1869, the Red Stockings spent $71.73 on gymnasium training that year.[7]

It was never too early to start training, either. Half a dozen of the Pittsburgh Alleghenys, namely Pud Galvin, Sam Barkley, George Miller, Charles Smith, Bill Bishop, and Bill Kuehne, entered the gymnasium to begin training for 1887 in early January.[8] (Incidentally, this shows that many players, between training and exhibition tours, really did make a year-round profession out of baseball, contradicting those who wanted to slash their salaries because they only "worked" six or seven months of the year.) Many players considered some gymnasium practice especially important in preparation for any season, but getting ready for the 1887 season was more important than most. That was the year that baseball's rules makers did away with the rule allowing the batter to call for a high or low pitch from the pitcher. Now, the pitcher could deliver the ball for a strike anywhere between the knees and armpits of the batter. Some hitters, used to calling for either a high or low pitch, spent hours in practice to make sure they could adapt to the change in regulations.

On rare occasions in the 1880s, entire clubs would enter the gymnasium together to get their work in before the season began. In 1887, St. Louis Browns owner Chris Von der Ahe instructed his players to arrive in town by March 10, so the players could trim down to their fighting weight, although some, such as outfielder Curt Welch, were early birds. Welch had been playing handball at Sportsman's Park since January.[9] Likewise, the Washington

Nationals got their marching orders to arrive during the first two weeks of March 1887, where the entire club took part in daily exercise.[10] Brooklyn owner Charles Byrne wanted his men in training by mid-March in 1887, stating that they would do their work under the careful eye of an experienced training specialist, Jack McMasters.[11]

This idea of hiring experts, or at least people who claimed to be experts, to train the nine seems a popular one. Pittsburgh, in their 1887 gymnasium work, considered engaging a well-known local sprinter named George Smith to work with its players on their baserunning form.[12] Likewise, when the Cleveland Blues entered their gymnasium preparatory to the 1887 season, "the men will all be here by March 20, and will at once be put into the Cleveland Athletic Club gymnasium on Frankfort street. There under the eye of James A. himself, and the hand of Dick Collier and Bob Bell, the gymnasium instructors, the men will go through a daily course of work suited to their positions, baths, and rubbing."[13]

Some players, of course, enjoyed training more than others. Baseball's premier player-mascot, outfielder Hugh Nicol, who "although small in stature, is a veritable Hercules in strength," demonstrated a devotion to conditioning himself and others. Once, he supposedly threw a 315-pound man in a wrestling match in late 1886 (although with a reported playing weight of 145 pounds, the reader can believe the tale or not) while he served as a professor at a gymnasium in Rockford, Illinois. He accepted a challenge from Cincinnati's "Kid" Baldwin for a wrestling match that same off-season (a good match because Baldwin had a playing weight of 147 pounds) and went into training with a noted wrestler known as "Strangler" Lewis to prepare himself properly.[14] Nicol said, "I am in first-class health, and feel like a race horse; I tip the beam at exactly 155 pounds, and am as stout as a bull."[15] The much-anticipated bout never took place, however. It seems Baldwin backed out at the last moment.[16]

Baldwin was another unpredictable character of 1880s baseball, which was often true of players who earned the sobriquet "Kid." The police arrested him once, along with fellow ballplayer Buck Ewing and 103 other spectators, for attending an illegal cockfight. His indiscretion cost him a $27 fine.[17] Another episode came in November of 1887 where, after some excess tippling in a Cincinnati saloon on Vine Street, he sustained a bloody nose when punched in the face by a local prizefighter. Baldwin invited the boxer "to the outside" where they duked it out in the streets. Baldwin got the best of the man, however, according to reports, so perhaps he declined to wrestle Hugh Nicol for reasons other than a fear of defeat.[18]

It was rare for a player to have exercise equipment or workout gear at his home, but a few men did. Shortstop Bill Gleason, who played in St. Louis, Philadelphia, and Louisville in the second half of the 1880s, was one such devotee to fitness and the gymnasium. He constructed his own workout room at his home in St. Louis and exercised constantly: "He walks and runs about fifteen miles every day, and he puts in the rest of his spare time handling Indian clubs, dumb-bells and other gymnasium apparatus. Bill has a little gymnasium of his own."[19]

Gleason's routine also gives us some idea of what players did while in training, even if not all the training methods would pass muster today. Walking or running, lifting dumbbells, playing handball, and other gymnasium exercises were nothing special to players in 1880s baseball. There were novel approaches by modern baseball training standards, as well. Washington Nationals pitcher Frank Gilmore took things to an extreme in his efforts to enhance his physique and improve his hitting for the 1888 season. In his attempt to bulk up, "he realizes that he can strengthen and harden those muscles brought into play while batting by the judicious use of Indian war clubs for a brief period daily, without reducing or impairing his ability as a pitcher."[20] An Indian war club was a club with a ball-shaped end to add weight, so using one was like swinging a bat but with the weight of the object distributed more unevenly.

Perhaps Gilmore figured that, with a career batting average of .049 entering 1888, things could only get better, but incredibly, his club-swinging routine hurt his performance at bat. He got just one hit in forty-one tries in 1888, for a .024 batting mark. He left major league baseball after that season, boasting a career batting average of .043 in 163 trips to the plate.

Although probably a good practice, all things considered, not all players liked gymnasium work, and if the team did not handle this situation correctly, this had the potential of generating discord in the ranks, or rancor between players and management, even before the championship season began. When discussing the prospects of entering the gymnasium for training in mid-March for 1887, John Morrill, the captain of the Boston Beaneaters, noted that workhorse pitcher Charlie Radbourn wanted nothing to do with such things as preparatory training. Morrill said of Radbourn, "He don't think much of it, and don't care to begin work until he can get out on the diamond." Morrill was not overly distressed in Radbourn's case, however, noting, "He looks as though he could step in to-morrow and pitch through a game without the slightest inconvenience. Fishing, hunting and quiet living have done good work for the great twirler this winter."[21]

Similarly indisposed toward gymnasium practice was Louisville's notoriously intoxicated outfielder Pete Browning. Browning once said, "Old Pete's no sucker; he wasn't raised in Morehead, and he hain't goin' up against any of them dod-gasted pulleys or put on any of them damn sweaters until he's got to. When the sun shines on both sides of the fence Pete, old boy, will be there, teaching all the guys how to line 'em out."[22] In order to reduce player hostility toward a training regimen they might not agree with, Manager Gus Schmelz, in Cincinnati's employ by 1887, tried to set a personal example of proper training for his men to reduce their animosity over reporting for duty in mid-March: "This will mean real gymnasium work for them, as their manager is 'stuck' on that sort of preparatory training, and works as hard himself as if he were preparing for the diamond himself instead of merely coaching."[23]

For every Radbourn or Browning, however, baseball had players like pitcher Ed Morris. Morris, in fact, went to extreme lengths to ready himself for the 1888 season. After a disappointing 1887 campaign in which his performance dropped off considerably because rule changes regarding the delivery of pitches, plus sore arm troubles, hurt his work in the pitcher's box, he vowed to get in shape to redeem himself. In a move about as extreme as a ballplayer could undertake in the Gilded Age, he swore off spirituous liquors and joined the local Young Men's Christian Association, although "He has not, however, become religious, his object in joining the association being to get the use of its gymnasium."[24] While "the rumor that Ed has joined the temperance army is a little premature," Morris claimed "he will take the pledge on New Year's Day, however, and he means to keep it."[25] Morris, true to his word, did so.[26] He also commenced an outdoor fitness program: "Morris is taking long walks daily to reduce his weight, with great success. His clothes are already too big for him. He has dropped 14 pounds since he started."[27]

Although gymnasium training was the accepted and most common way to work into form in the 1880s, a few rebel managers disdained it. Philadelphia Quakers leader Harry Wright was one. He preferred a tour of exhibition games, and had little interest in the gymnasium except as a last resort: "It is not the present intention to put the Phillies to gymnasium practice. 'Give me ten day's practice in the field,' says Mr. Wright, 'and the other teams can have their month's practice in a gymnasium. In my opinion one day on the field is nearly as good as one week in a gymnasium.'"[28] He got his way in 1887 when his club embarked on a Southern trip, beginning in Charleston on March 26.[29] One top player, Harry Stovey, agreed with his manager, stating, "A couple of days in the field will do more for a player than a month in a gymnasium or rink."[30]

One thing a team could do that resembled gymnasium training but probably was more fun for the players was playing handball. By 1888, many baseball observers believed this was the very best way to prepare during the off-season. Cap Anson in Chicago played frequently. Brooklyn's management, absolutely convinced of handball's virtues, engaged the court at the Brooklyn Hand Ball Club in the mornings during March and April of 1888 to limber up their nine. Not only that, they also paid for "the services of champion Phil Casey to train the players in hand ball each morning while field practice is not available and on rainy days in the early spring months. Terry has been training this way for some weeks already, and he has gained the greatest advantage in it."[31]

Physical training of some kind was especially important for older players hoping to hold time at bay for one more year and stay in the game. Third baseman Ezra Sutton of Boston was one such player. Born in Seneca Falls, New York, in 1849, just one year after the famed Seneca Falls Convention for women's rights, by 1887 Sutton was a grizzled veteran looking to convince onlookers he still belonged on the diamond. His hitting talent remained obvious, but during the 1886 season his defensive range came under fire from newspaper observers in Boston. He might have countered that the club tried to play him in the outfield part of the time, where he had played all of eight games in his career up to that point. Regardless, Sutton tried to reassure the doubters in the winter of 1886-1887 by sending frequent letters to friends in the Boston press, describing his advanced state of fitness achieved through working at his sawmill in Palmyra, New York.[32] Tim Murnane reported that, when the Boston club went into gymnasium that spring, Sutton was the hardest worker present, and that "he looks just as young today" as when he first broke into baseball with the Cleveland and Middletown, Connecticut, clubs in the early 1870s.[33] Murnane would know because he was also a member of the Middletown Mansfields, posting a .360 batting average as the team's first baseman in 1872.

Another option, besides entering a gymnasium in the Northern states to prepare for the season at hand, was a tour of the South, playing exhibition matches against local nines and minor league teams. The White Stockings, we noted earlier, liked Hot Springs, Arkansas, as their training ground. The Detroit Wolverines went farther south in 1887, staying at the Hotel Lanier in Macon, Georgia, starting on March 8. Their plan was to train there on the local grounds for ten days, play some practice games with the Macon semi-pro team, then play exhibition games at Mobile, New Orleans, Savannah, Charleston, Birmingham, Decatur, Memphis, Nashville, and Louisville, ending their tour in the Falls City on April 15. Not satisfied with this slate of games, the Wolverines decided to hold more games against northern competition after the 15th, and scheduled some additional games with La Crosse, Minneapolis, St. Paul, and finally Milwaukee, a trip of nearly two months covering about 4,000 miles.[34] Often, such games were not very competitive, especially when featuring teams with the strength of Detroit, but they were good practice for the major league team and a chance to see major league baseball for baseball fans in the South who would probably never see major league baseball otherwise. The Wolverines played twenty-three games on their tour and won all of them, most easily, although the Memphis club lost by a single tally on two occasions.[35]

Not all clubs thought that a Southern tour was a good idea, however, often for financial reasons. That same spring, 1887, Pittsburgh eschewed a trip south because "there is no money in it," instead deciding to tough out the colder April weather in the Smoky City and play a series of games against Syracuse, Buffalo, Toronto, and Utica. Pittsburgh manager Horace Phillips believed fourteen games against these clubs would give his nine plenty of time to shake off whatever rust had accumulated over the winter.[36] Pittsburgh's ownership, recognizing the need for something to help its team in the early months of the year, however, considered the idea of constructing a state of the art gymnasium on its grounds at

Recreation Park: "A handsome building will be erected at Recreation Park, in which there will be a complete gymnasium outfit, together with bowling alleys, tennis courts, etc. A cinder path for spring runners and cyclists will be provided."[37]

Still others could not decide if touring the Sun Belt was the right decision or not because they recognized both the value and drawbacks of preseason travel. Jack Kerins of Louisville, when asked in 1888 if a Southern trip worked to the team's advantage, confessed that he was not sure: "We never make any money by them. In fact we usually lose a little, but I suppose they serve a good purpose in taking the kinks out of the boys' muscles, and forcing them to overcome the stiffness of their winter rest. But still this exercise is sometimes injurious, as it may be too early and too severe. There have been many cases in which a man has been injured for an entire season by it."[38]

Even if taking an exhibition tour did not pay, however, financially speaking it was better than traveling to some Southern locale to work into shape. In 1887, the Chicago White Stockings debated whether they should repeat their 1886 trip to Hot Springs, Arkansas. The team's captain, Cap Anson, preferred the idea, but owner Al Spalding did not.

Anson and Spalding cannot agree respecting the best plan. Spalding is of the opinion that a series of games in the South will conduce more to a better playing condition than a boiling out at Hot Springs, while Anson favors the latter idea. Anson opposes a Southern trip from his past experience, for the club never returned from such an expedition without several of the players being crippled. Spalding opposes a journey to the Springs, owing to the heavy expenses incurred, while if they took a Southern trip they could pay for the expense of their training.[39]

Based on prior experience, Anson believed that playing a heavy slate of exhibition games ran the risk of getting players banged up and injured before the championship season even began, thus handicapping the White Stockings unnecessarily. Team owner Spalding, in contrast, tended to favor a tour of games because while the team might not profit from these games financially, the players got live practice and the club lost less money for its time and effort. A trip to Hot Springs or some other training ground offered little remuneration to the club, and Spalding figured that losing a little money was better than losing a lot of money.[40] In 1887, at least, Anson's views prevailed, and the White Stockings traveled south to Hot Springs just as they had the previous year. Spalding's quote is interesting, however, because it shows that the idea of holding spring training very nearly died after just one year. Given Spalding's reputation in baseball circles, any other club was sure to think twice before attempting something he had rejected.

Like Anson and others realized, besides the monetary considerations, playing too many exhibition games risked injury to important members of a nine before the season even began. John Morrill, a player and captain for the Boston Beaneaters, had exactly this in mind when he decided against a tour of the South in 1887. When the team returned from their 1886 series of exhibitions, second baseman Jack Burdock had a bad leg, third baseman Billy Nash a sprained ankle, utility player Sam Wise an injured arm, pitcher Charlie Buffinton a bad arm, and utility player Ezra Sutton contracted malaria. As a result, as of the end of May, the team's record was a pathetic 6 wins, 17 losses. The rest of the season, after the injured players healed up, the Beaneaters were a respectable 50 wins versus 44 losses. Morrill also said that in future travels, he would lean more on the new players and give the older, more established players more time off. His preferred method of preparation was the gymnasium, and he blamed the injuries of '86 on too little time working out before taking the field.[41] The Philadelphia Athletics of the American Association felt the same way. They, too, entered the gymnasium known as the Elite Rink in

March of 1887, rather than go on a tour, in order that they would have "no lame arms, sore shoulders or other defects in the players."[42]

Even if a team decided to play exhibition games and tour the South, it had to be careful on the schedule and timing of its Southern tour, according to Harry Wright. One reason he declined to head to the Sun Belt before the 1888 season was that while "he has not lost faith in the beneficial effect of the Southern climate and knows of no better means of getting into condition," he feared to return to Philadelphia too early and leave too many days between his time spent in the South and the opening of the season. This was because "the transition from the warm South to the North at a time when the latter has not yet entirely shaken off its winter garb, is hazardous and calculated not only to immediately undo all the work accomplished by again stiffening up the men, but it is apt to render them more than ordinarily liable to colds and inflammations."[43]

Perhaps, as Northerners moving into the Southern climate, they were more vulnerable to malaria as well. The Mason-Dixon Line is the approximate boundary north of which mosquitoes carrying the *Plasmodium vivex* form of malaria cannot infect people, due to insufficient temperatures. While doctors knew what malaria was and how to treat it (quinine from the bark of the cinchona tree) by this time, they did not learn that mosquitoes were the infection vector until somewhat later.[44] One baseball veteran observed that "there is a good deal more danger of sickness coming upon a player who has been South and returned than there is to the one who remains North and goes into such preliminary practice in his native climate."[45]

For 1888, then, Wright and his men instead headed for Cape May, New Jersey, where "he routs every man of them out at six o'clock, and they give each other salt water baths with water just brought in from the cold surf. Vigorous rubbing with rough towels follows and at half-past six the squads start off for a thirty minute brisk walk over the beach to the Government life station."[46] They did all this work under the watchful eye of Trainer Taylor, with the result that "the men are gradually reducing" their winter stores of flesh.[47]

While physical training and exhibition tours were popular ways to prepare for the season, players tried other, less scientific, things to try to stay in condition. Reflecting the marginal medical knowledge of the day, patent medicines, unfortunately, figured in the training regimens of some players. For instance, Ed Swartwood, primarily an outfielder who played in the American Association in the 1880s, praised the benefits of *cascara sagrada*, a laxative obtained from tree bark, as an all-purpose weight loss drug: "This remedy is easy and sure, and if Bill Taylor and Hardie Henderson took a dose every day for three weeks then they could truthfully say to all the world: 'I'm in great favor.' It beats walking all hollow, for all you have to do is to take a few doses daily and sit down and watch the fat evaporate."[48] (We have already met Billy Taylor, and Hardie Henderson was another promising pitcher whose career ended prematurely because of his inability to lay off the fire water.)

The players most likely to sustain serious injury in 1880s baseball were pitchers and catchers, which is part of the reason why they often received higher pay than other players. Throwing a baseball at high velocity is a very stressful thing for the arm's muscles. The history of the game in the 1880s and beyond abounds with pitchers who performed admirably for a few seasons but then suffered serious arm injuries and had to leave major league baseball due to those injuries reducing their effectiveness. This was especially true in the late 1880s, when a typical team featured three main pitchers, with maybe a fourth or fifth man who pitched here and there (observers referred to them as "change pitchers"), and pitchers generally pitched the entire game, no matter how many innings it might last or pitches they might throw. It was quite common for a team's best pitcher to start 40 to 50 games in a championship season, sometimes more, and that does not even count the many exhibition games teams played that do not register in official statistics. In 1887, just to pick one year, five National

League pitchers worked more than 400 innings. The only thing mitigating some of the stress this imposed on pitchers was that home plate was not yet sixty feet, six inches from the pitcher, that change coming in 1893.

Because of this level of work, pitchers sustained arm injuries frequently, and pitchers who developed sore arms tried any number of things to cure their ailments and get back into the pitcher's box. One of the most popular "cures" for a sore pitching arm was a brief shock of electricity. Several pitchers employed this tactic. In 1887, Pittsburgh pitcher Ed Morris said, "My arm is in good shape again. . . . I think electricity did it much good. The doctor gave me a dose that knocked me off a chair. He said a woman could stand two cells and he gave me forty-two."[49]

Also in 1887, former pitcher Fred Goldsmith tried a much more extreme remedy to get his arm back in condition. Having last pitched in the majors in 1884, out of desperation he submitted to the Moxa treatment, which meant, "he has had the muscles of his arm blistered with a hot iron, similar to the treatment used on the strained tendons of race-horses."[50] It did not work, at least not to the point where any major league teams were willing to sign him. Still not willing to face the inevitable, by 1888 Goldsmith was in Hot Springs, Arkansas, hoping the supposed curative properties of the local waters would do the trick for him. Because the Chicago White Stockings also trained at Hot Springs, he hoped to impress Chicago's Cap Anson and get a shot at a contract that way, however unlikely that seemed on a White Stockings club that had already signed about twenty men that winter. The waters did not help, sadly, any more than the hot iron did, and he never again pitched in major league baseball.[51] He stayed in the game, however, serving as a substitute umpire in the American Association in 1888 and a regular umpire the next year until losing his position for his role in the notorious 1889 Brooklyn-St. Louis fiasco described in chapter thirteen.[52]

Louisville thought it had a better answer for sore arms than electricity or hot irons. In 1887, the club employed "Professor"

William Patterson, noted for his faith in the virtues of magnetic healing: "He has treated the arms of Hecker, Chamberlain and Ramsey with great success, and restored each to good condition when the aspects were very discouraging." Patterson had so much luck (one hesitates to use words such as skill or success) treating the Louisville pitching staff that the team considered employing him on a full-time basis to keep its nine in good condition for 1888.[53]

With all these risks to pitchers, it made sense that those hurlers with a reputation for durability were in high demand. In November of 1887, the Cleveland Blues signed a new pitcher, Edward Bakley, away from the Rochester club. *The Sporting News* described the transaction by noting that Bakley "has plenty of speed and skill, and never has a sore arm."[54] The description was apt, at least for 1888, because Bakley started 61 games for the Blues that season and logged 532 innings in the pitcher's box.

Catchers were also at great risk. The practice of wearing a glove to catch pitches caught on slowly throughout the decade, but the gloves were primitive. Even with a glove, therefore, the catcher's hands were only a stray pitch or foul tip away from jammed or broken fingers. Without much other protective gear, foul balls often hit various parts of the catcher's body as well, with all the bumps, bruises, and broken bones one would expect on seeing the human body struck by a solid object traveling eighty or more miles per hour. Catchers, like umpires, were starting to wear masks for protection, but like the gloves, these early masks had design limitations and only partially fulfilled their purpose of protecting the face. To cite just a few of the many examples regarding their marginal effectiveness, in 1887 a foul tip struck Louisville catcher Lave Cross and "glanced his mask and peeled off a portion of the scalp. The wound bled freely, but Cross pluckily finished the game." Part of the reason Cross was in the game in the first place was that Louisville manager John Kelly had another of the club's backstops, John Kerins, guarding first base because the team needed his bat, but Kerins's hands were too tender to catch pitches.[55]

Similarly, that same year the New York Metropolitans struggled to keep a full complement of catchers healthy: "Catchers Holbert and Sommers are disabled, and Donahue is the only catcher left. Either Rooney Sweeney or Tom Deasley will be pressed into service."[56] This shows that having three catchers on hand was an absolute minimum, with four preferred. Like New York, in 1889, the Kansas City Cowboys found themselves in similar straits: "Jimmy Donohue is all out of shape just now, and is unable to catch. Reynolds' hands, too, are sore, and Gunson is not in the best of trim. Consequently Hoover is compelled to do most of the back stopping."[57]

Like pitchers, some catchers earned a reputation for durability, and along with a catcher's ability to handle pitchers, durability, even more than hitting talent, tended to make or break the catcher's reputation with the press. Take Doc Bushong, for instance. He had a reputation for catching regularly and being especially durable. In 1888, he played in just 69 of Brooklyn's 140 games, but that was still good enough to place second in the American Association for games caught that season. In 1885 and 1886, he led the Association in games caught both seasons, catching in 191 of St. Louis's 251 games in those two years. In fact, in 1886, Bushong became the first catcher to catch 100 games in a championship season, going behind the bat 106 times.

Because of these risks, men who could take the abuse were always in demand. Hoping to find a dependable man to spell Charlie Bennett as catcher in 1888, the Detroit Wolverines signed Cal Broughton, in large part because of his constitution: "He is just the man that is wanted to catch Conway, who is the hardest of all the Detroit pitchers to handle. Broughton is a man that can stand any amount of punishment, and the chances are that he will have an opportunity to make a martyr of himself."[58] This is why newspapers often made a big deal of things when a catcher caught several games in a row, while they rarely did so for other players. It was hard to stay healthy for long when going behind the bat; thus, any streak that exceeded ten games or so merited mention for being exceptional.

Besides injury, other things could ruin a player's physical condition. Off-field incidents occurred with distressing frequency as well. Fights brought on by excessive alcohol consumption were foremost among these, as we noted in chapters one and two. Accidents happened, too, such as when one player had his hand pecked while preening one of his trained fighting birds. One other important issue, barely hinted at in the press, given the straight-laced public morals of the Gilded Age, was the visitation of prostitutes and the resultant risk of sexually transmitted disease. Baseball players were, as a group, certainly in the high-risk category for this affliction. Although no one mentioned this vice by name in baseball chronicles, professional ballplayers were in the prime of life, sometimes married but often not, frequently on the road for long stretches away from their families or friends, often intoxicated, and almost completely immersed in an environment valuing "manly" traits such as physical and sexual prowess, with the resultant peer pressure to conform to group expectations.

We must thank sportswriter O. P. Caylor for having the nerve to bring up this topic in print. While never quite using words such as *prostitute* explicitly, and certainly not naming any specific players guilty of this behavior, he discussed the issue in an 1887 column for *The Sporting Life*. He wrote, "It is an evil which cannot be discussed in public prints as it deserves. I refer to disease which players so often contract and which, if it does not wholly destroy them as ball players, unfits them in their profession for months." He continued, "Many notable cases of this kind could be cited; and dozens of cases of 'malaria,' 'sprains' and 'Charley-horses' so-called have been nothing else but a shrewd invention or pretension to hide from the management the diseased condition of the player who has found himself in a physical form which wholly unfits him for doing his duty to the club and earning his salary."[59] It was Caylor's belief that "this evil is a more general one than is commonly imagined, and

108

though it has broken up some of the best and most important players in the various clubs, it is confined almost entirely to the lower strata of the profession" who "seek the dangerous society of the class of people from whom these evils are contracted, and who are found after night on the prominent streets of large cities looking for victims among such men whose desires it does not take much in the way of physical temptation to excite." He ended with the apologetically worded statement, "It is the most destructive form of intemperance with which the profession has to deal, and I may therefore be excused if my pen has dealt with it too plainly," but also suggested that each club "have at its call the services of a reputable physician to whom every member of the team shall be sent for examination. So soon as any of these cases of malaria, sprains or Charley-horse begin to develop, and from the day that such player becomes unfit to fully do his professional duty by reason of the disease named he should have his salary shut off."[60]

The Methuselah of baseball writers, Henry Chadwick, supported Caylor on this matter. He stated, regarding players maintaining their condition over the course of a season, "over-eating is bad, excessive drinking is worse, but the worst of all is the dissipation of the habitués of brothels. Many of the serious sicknesses of players last season was due to this latter cause. Caylor has done a good thing in calling attention to it. As manager of two teams he knows whereof he speaks."[61] Later, Chadwick repeated this belief, although, regrettably, he did not provide many precise details: "The saloon and the brothel are the evils of the base ball world at the present day; and we see it practically exemplified in the failure of noted players to play up to the standard they are capable of were they to avoid these gross evils."[62] Because Chadwick also edited Al Spalding's yearly baseball guides, it was no surprise when the 1889 guide stated, "The two great obstacles in the way of the success of the majority of professional ball players are wine and women. The saloon and the brothel are the evils of the baseball world at the present day."[63]

A few other sources corroborate Caylor and Chadwick. For example, just prior to the 1888 season, one of the Cincinnati Red Stockings, catcher John O'Connor, got himself into trouble on this score: "John O'Connor, one of Cincinnati's catchers, was arrested the other day and fined $15 and costs for drunkenness. A disreputable woman caused his arrest."[64] Likewise, when the Philadelphia Athletics saw several members of their nine drinking heavily in 1888, some of the men "kept late hours and still others consorted with women to such an extent that they became too enervated to even stop a thrown ball on the bound."[65]

Although men like Caylor and Chadwick believed the problem widespread, mentions in the press like those just described were quite rare. Pittsburgh manager Horace Phillips explained part of the reason why so few cases came to light. Team managers often shielded their players from the unwanted attention because if word got out regarding the company some players kept, the damage to the team's, and baseball's, reputation would be immense. The "respectable" fans each club wanted to court would hardly attend games if they thought the men they watched play were all drunkards, gamblers, or associates of loose women. The only reason Phillips revealed even this much was that he was angry with one player he had shielded from such unwanted attention in the past because that player ungratefully pressed Phillips for more money in salary negotiations: "There is one man whom I have protected in many a scrape and kept it away from the newspapers, and in reward he abuses me. Why, I found him in the grand stand in New York with a well-known woman whom he had represented to be his sister, and the boys know there are dozens of other scrapes in which matters have been kept quiet through my efforts."[66]

Usually, teams succeeded in keeping the sexual habits of their players out of the news for the reasons described by Phillips, but not always. Just before the 1889 season opened, two Columbus players, pitcher Bill Widner and outfielder Ed Daily, decided to examine the nightlife in Baltimore, causing one writer to comment, "Columbus is already on another voyage of discovery. Widner and Daily made a scientific investigation that occupied all of Tuesday night. In the morning, at the urgent request of Manager Buckenberger, they contributed fifty dollars each to the club coffers." At first, observers surmised that the men must have been guilty of a drinking spree because Buckenberger had promulgated a strict code of conduct for his team that called for a fifty-dollar fine for the first drinking infraction. Buckenberger decided to clear his players on the drinking charge but in the process had to own up to what the men had really done: "Buck says but for this one indiscretion the boys are all behaving themselves as well as he could desire, and he wants it distinctly understood that Daily and Widner are not drinking, but in this case were a little too susceptible to female charms, and he thought it prudent to check it for once and all time."[67]

After putting out this fire, Buckenberger soon had his hands full with drinking players as well, with pitcher John Weyhing earning a suspension for lushing during the first week of the season. According to one of the sportswriters following the team, he should have known better than to attempt to hide his infraction: "Columbus has had so many drinking bum ball players on her salary list in the past years it is too late in the base ball day for any player to think now that we don't know a lush when we see one."[68] Buckenberger's conduct reminds us, however, that any number of things might ruin a ballplayer's health in Gilded Age baseball, whether it was injuries, alcohol, or sexually transmitted diseases. A wise manager had to stay on the lookout for any of these possibilities.

Clearly, the 1880s were a time of transition for major league baseball when it came to the issue of how to get players in good condition and keep them there. Teams were still working out the answer to questions like whether it was better to go on an exhibition tour, hold spring training at a designated spot, or just stay home and wait for the weather to get better. They also faced the problem of trying to have enough good men on hand to replace injured players, especially the pitchers and catchers, as well as how to treat men when injury occurred. All these questions and answers linked back to the two central considerations of team owners: how to win games and make money. As much as teams experimented with the best ways to keep their men healthy, this question continued vexing them because it had no clear answer.

---

[1] Remlap, "Remlap's Letter," *The Sporting Life*, April 14, 1886, 5.

[2] Henry Chadwick, "Chadwick's Chat," *The Sporting Life*, February 6, 1889, 3.

[3] H. E. K., "The White Stockings," *The Sporting News*, March 17, 1886, 1.

[4] Harry Palmer, "From Chicago," *The Sporting Life*, March 9, 1887, 4. Palmer, just like many other writers of the time, turned the word "white" into an adjective to describe a person's honesty. This is a not-too-subtle reminder of the power and pervasiveness of racism in Gilded Age baseball.

[5] "Notes and Comments," *The Sporting Life*, September 7, 1887, 3.

[6] Eli, "The Chicago Players," *The Sporting News*, March 26, 1887, 5.

[7] "The Quaker City," *The Sporting News*, February 19, 1887, 1.

[8] C. M. B., "From the Smoky City," *The Sporting Life*, January 12, 1887, 1.

[9] Pritchard, "From St. Louis," *The Sporting Life*, January 12, 1887, 2.

[10] "The Capital City Team," *The Sporting News*, January 15, 1887, 5.

[11] "The Brooklyn Team," *The Sporting News*, February 12, 1887, 1.

[12] C. M. B., "From the Smoky City," *The Sporting Life*, February 16, 1887, 1.

[13] F. H. Brunell, "From Cleveland," *The Sporting Life*, February 16, 1887, 2. James A. was Cleveland manager Jimmy Williams.

[14] "Base Ball Wrestlers," *The Sporting Life*, January 5, 1887, 1.

[15] Pritchard, "From St. Louis," *The Sporting Life*, January 12, 1887, 2.

[16] O. P. Caylor, "From Cincinnati," *The Sporting Life*, January 19, 1887, 4.

[17] Ren Mulford, Jr., "From Cincinnati," *The Sporting Life*, February 16, 1887, 4.

[18] "The Kid and Jem Smith," *The Sporting News*, November 26, 1887, 1.

[19] Joe Pritchard, "St. Louis Siftings," *The Sporting Life*, February 29, 1888, 4.

[20] Bob Larner, "Washington Whispers" *The Sporting Life*, January 18, 1888, 6.

[21] Mugwump, "From the Hub," *The Sporting Life*, January 26, 1887, 2.

[22] "Notes and Comments," *The Sporting Life*, February 27, 1889, 4.

[23] "Notes and Comments," *The Sporting Life*, January 26, 1887, 3.

[24] "Among the Ball Tossers," *Chicago Daily Tribune*, December 18, 1887, 27.

[25] Circle, "Pittsburg Pencilings," *The Sporting Life*, December 28, 1887, 4.

[26] Circle, "Pittsburg Pencilings," *The Sporting Life*, January 11, 1888, 2.

[27] Circle, "Pittsburg Pencilings," *The Sporting Life*, January 18, 1888, 6.

[28] "The Quaker City," *The Sporting News*, February 19, 1887, 1.

[29] "Local News," *The Sporting Life*, February 23, 1887, 5. The Philadelphia Quakers are the same team as today's Philadelphia Phillies. Officially, their team name was the Quakers through the 1889 season, although some started calling them the Phillies around this time. They changed their team name for the 1890 season.

[30] "Philadelphia News," *The Sporting Life*, April 13, 1887, 4.

[31] Henry Chadwick, "Chadwick's Chat," *The Sporting Life*, March 7, 1888, 3. Terry was pitcher Adonis Terry.

[32] "A Rattling Program," *The Sporting News*, January 22, 1887, 3.

[33] Tim Murnane, "Tim Murnane's Chaff," *The Sporting News*, April 2, 1887, 1.

[34] M. A. T., "Detroit's Programme," *The Sporting Life*, January 19, 1887, 1; M. A. T., "Detroit Dotlets," *The Sporting Life*, February 16, 1887, 4.

[35] M. A. T., "The Southern Trip Over," *The Sporting Life*, April 20, 1887, 5.

[36] C. M. B., "From the Smoky City," *The Sporting Life*, January 19, 1887, 1.

[37] "Notes and Comments," *The Sporting Life*, January 26, 1887, 3.

[38] J. A., "Louisville Laconics," *The Sporting Life*, December 26, 1888, 5.

[39] "What Shall the Harvest Be," *The Sporting Life*, February 16, 1887, 4.

[40] Ibid.

[41] Mugwump, "From the Hub," *The Sporting Life*, January 26, 1887, 2.

[42] "The Philadelphia Players," *The Sporting News*, March 5, 1887, 1.

[43] "Philadelphia Pointers," *The Sporting Life*, February 22, 1888, 2.

[44] Charles Mann, *1493: Uncovering the New World Columbus Created*, (New York: Alfred A. Knopf, 2011). See chapter three for more details about malaria and the United States.

[45] O. P. Caylor, "Caylor's Comment," *The Sporting Life*, February 29, 1888, 3.

[46] "The Philadelphia Team at Work," *The Sporting News*, March 31, 1888, 1.

[47] Quaker, "The Quaker City," *The Sporting News*, March 31, 1888, 1.

[48] Circle, "Pittsburg Pencilings," *The Sporting Life*, March 27, 1889, 5.

[49] Circle, "Pittsburg Pointers," *The Sporting Life*, September 21, 1887, 4.

[50] "Notes and Comments," *The Sporting Life*, April 27, 1887, 11.

[51] "Notes and Comments," *The Sporting Life*, February 22, 1888, 5; M. A. T., "Detroit Dotlets," *The Sporting Life*, March 14, 1888, 2.

[52] "Goldsmith a Substitute Umpire," *The Sporting News*, July 28, 1888, 1.

[53] X. X., "From the Falls City," *The Sporting Life*, September 7, 1887, 4.

[54] "Cleveland Signs Bakley," *The Sporting News*, November 19, 1887, 1.

[55] X. X., "From the Falls City," *The Sporting Life*, September 7, 1887, 4.

[56] "The New York Clubs," *The Sporting Life*, September 14, 1887, 1.

[57] Freeman, "Less Exultant," *The Sporting Life*, May 22, 1889, 1.

[58] Dan, "The World's Champions," *The Sporting News*, December 10, 1887, 5.

[59] O. P. Caylor, "Caylor's Comment," *The Sporting Life*, November 9, 1887, 5.

[60] Ibid.

[61] Henry Chadwick, "Chadwick's Chat," *The Sporting Life*, December 7, 1887, 5.

[62] Henry Chadwick, "Chadwick's Chat," *The Sporting Life*, November 14, 1888, 3. Methuselah was a biblical figure who reputedly lived to be 969 years old. Chadwick was not that old by this time, of course, but had been involved in baseball since the 1840s.

[63] *Spalding's Official 1889 Base Ball Guide*, 58.

[64] "Notes and Comments," *The Sporting Life*, February 22, 1888, 5.

[65] "Philadelphia Pointers," *The Sporting Life*, September 5, 1888, 6.

[66] Circle, "Pittsburg Pencilings," *The Sporting Life*, November 21, 1888, 3.

[67] T. T. T., "Baltimore Bulletin," *The Sporting Life*, April 24, 1889, 5. I was unable to discover whether Widner's nickname, "Wild Bill," comes from his behavior off the field or his control of the ball while pitching, but given that his career walk rate was a very reasonable 2.4 per nine innings, it appears that the former is more likely.

[68] F. W. Arnold, "Columbus Chatter" *The Sporting Life*, May 1, 1889, 5.

Chapter 5

Cheating and Dishonest Play

In any sport with rules, some always those who seek to bend, and even break, the rules to gain a competitive advantage over the opposition, and Gilded Age baseball players were no exception. They had sundry opportunities for cheating, and the temptation to win often overruled the better angels of the players' natures. In fact, ballplayers broke the rules frequently, brazenly, and, sometimes, very creatively. The modern reader, used to seeing baseball players cheat by taking steroids to bulk up their physiques, and maybe trying to steal the signs of the other team, might think the number of things baseball players got away with in the 1880s bewildering. How were they able to cheat so much?

The reason, it turns out, is simple. The most important factor that allowed for so much cheating was the cheapness of team owners. In the 1880s, just one umpire patrolled the field. The expectation was that this man could see everything, or at least enough things that the game would run smoothly, the players would not argue, and the game might proceed in an orderly, dignified fashion. This did not always happen. In fact, it was rare. Instead, many players, aware of the wide assortment of rules in baseball, broke those rules whenever the umpire turned his back. As a result, some baseball observers started discussing the idea of having two umpires on the field at once. They called this idea the double umpire system. By the end of the decade, nearly everyone realized that one man, no matter how qualified and attentive, could not see everything. The only thing standing in the way of the double umpire system was the reluctance of team owners to spend the money and hire a second man. Having two umpires instead of one meant costs for umpires would double, and in the 1880s, team owners proved reluctant to spend the necessary money to assure honest play.

As a result, cheating and otherwise bending the rules was common, and it took many forms. Billy Taylor, besides enjoying a cold one, also enjoyed pulling a fast one whenever the situation looked promising. One writer remarked, "Few will forget Billy Taylor's trick of standing outside the coach lines and having the ball thrown to him on the claim that it was ripped, allowing it to pass and the man on third to come home. Taylor is the first man who was also known to score a run without going nearer than 20 feet of the base. He cuts across the field whenever the opportunity is offered."[1] This was not the only story about Billy Taylor's cheating, either. In another game Taylor went toward second base, where a close tag play awaited him. Instead of sliding into the base and into second baseman Joe Quest's tag, Taylor ran into the second baseman instead and wrestled with him a moment, causing Quest to muff the throw. Before anyone could notice, Taylor grabbed the ball and secreted it in his pocket, then proceeded to run all the way home and score while the rest of the players searched for the ball.[2]

Many others copied Taylor in his unsportsmanlike feat of cutting corners on the bases. Mike Kelly did so frequently, but the practice was common enough by 1887 that National League president Nick Young warned umpires to watch for the occurrence in his written instructions to them for that season. Young's missive also called for umpires' alertness regarding two other common tricks. One was when, on a ground ball to an infielder, the pitcher would cross the first base line in the name of backing up first base, but would do so just as the batter ran past, thereby disrupting the batter on his way to first. The other was the sleight of hand practiced by catchers whereby they would catch a pitch that was off the plate but almost imperceptibly move their glove back over the plate while catching the ball, making a ball appear to be a strike. This practice, known today as framing the pitch, allowed catchers, players, and fans to call the umpire's judgment into question, and Young wanted his arbiters to keep their attention on the location of the pitch and avoid this subterfuge.[3]

Another part of dishonest play was distracting the opposition while they tried to perform, and this also occurred frequently. One trick was the practice of a player on the batting team yelling confusing instructions to the outfielders as they attempted to catch a fly ball that was about halfway between them. With both men concentrating on tracking the ball through the air, and usually having to worry about not stumbling over ruts and potholes in the outfield as well because most teams' fields were in poor condition, the outfielders often had to depend on verbal signals from their teammates on who should take the ball. The offensive team might yell some signals of their own, hoping to confuse the defenders enough that the ball would fall in for a hit or, even worse, that the outfielders would collide with each other. Baltimore Orioles pitcher Matt Kilroy got himself ejected from a game for precisely this practice in early August of 1889.[4] That same year, umpire John Gaffney tossed Baltimore's Tommy Tucker from a game on May 28 for doing the same thing.[5]

Outfielders had their ways of striking back, however. Few were more devious, it seems, than Hugh Nicol. Some baseball observers considered Nicol the luckiest man in the game, and he was also among the craftiest. When he played right field for the St. Louis Browns, he perfected a trick later copied by Jim O'Rourke of the New York Giants and many others. Because Sportsman's Park in St.

Louis had benches with seats in the outfield, rather than an outfield fence, during Nicol's tenure in the Mound City,

> Hugh would report for duty every morning, and before he left the park for his dinner he would place a couple, and sometimes three balls under the right field seats, and he knew just where to find them, too, when necessity demanded it. When a batsman of an opposing nine knocked the ball under the right field seats Hugh would go over the inside fence in a twinkle, grasp the hidden ball, and before the runner could reach second, 'Robbie' would be waiting on the line, ball in hand, to retire him. Of course Captain Comiskey was not on to the scheme, and he has often purchased Nicol a good cigar after the game on account of his quick movements in returning the ball to the diamond.[6]

At times, entire teams developed a reputation for their creative approach to following the rules. In the heat of the 1886 pennant race between his New York team, Detroit, and Chicago, someone asked New York captain John Ward which team was more difficult to defeat. His answer reveals much about dishonest and rough play.

> Chicago, of course. All you have to do to beat Detroit is to play better ball than they do. To down the Chicagos, however, you have not only to play good ball, which is hard to do when playing with them, as they are continually attracting your attention by their tricks, but you must also watch them or they won't go near second or third base. Besides this, they rattle the umpire and the opposing nine by their 'bulldozing' tactics.[7]

Similarly, after Mike Kelly left Chicago to play in Boston in 1887, an interviewer asked him what was the strongest point of the Chicago nine. While admitting the team still had a terrific infield, which deserved much of the credit for the team's success, Kelly also said, "The Chicagos can beat any nine in the country at cunning and maneuvers."[8] Indeed, it was difficult to find anyone in 1880s baseball who believed Chicago was not the best in this regard: "Old-time players will tell you that Chicago has generally played a rough-and-tumble game for years; in fact, has won the championship on it frequently. Many umpires will permit the Chicago Club to do it."[9]

The American Association's answer to Chicago was the St. Louis Browns. Equally infamous for their rough and dishonest play, the Browns' tactics mirrored the attitude of their captain, first baseman Charlie Comiskey, who once said, "I go on a field to win a game by any hook or crook. It is the game we are after, not reputations as society dudes." Comiskey did not always like fighting or brawling but believed in bending the rules as far as they would stretch, then bending them a little more.[10] The unholy trinity of Comiskey and teammates Bill Gleason and Arlie Latham was the inspiration for baseball installing a box on the field for coaches. Recall that in the 1880s, "coaching" was not about instructing your own men, but about rattling the opposition. Baseball's rules makers decided to put down chalk lines to limit where coachers could stand because

> Comiskey and Bill Gleason used to plant themselves on each side of the visiting catcher and comment on his breeding, personal habits, skill as a receiver, or rather lack of it, until the unlucky backstop was unable to tell whether one or a dozen balls were coming his way. . . . So for the sake of not increasing the population of the insane asylums or encouraging justifiable homicide, the coach's box was invented. This helped out the catcher, but the pitcher and other players on the opposing team were still at the mercy of Comiskey, and I know of no man who had a sharper tongue, who was in command of more biting sarcasm, or who was quicker at repartee.[11]

Sadly, because Comiskey and Anson excelled at this practice, and their teams were winners, others decided to copy them. As a result, the game of the 1890s was probably even worse than baseball in the 1880s in this regard.

Even if observers acknowledged the White Stockings and Browns as masters of manipulation, trickery, and bulldozing, John Ward's New York team had a few tricks up its collective sleeves, too. By the mid-1880s the team had several veterans well-versed in baseball's arts of chicanery. In an exhibition game with the Washington Nationals in 1885, the left fielder for the Giants, Jim O'Rourke, came under suspicion for trying to introduce an unofficial ball into play. In the first inning of the game, with New York in the field, Washington's players (the home team was responsible for supplying the baseballs) detected a ball in play that was not the official ball they had presented. Soon players discovered that O'Rourke had concealed a ball in his shirt. He would not produce the ball or leave the field, however, and his manager, Jim Mutrie, backed his outfielder when O'Rourke claimed the ball was his personal property. Washington's manager Mike Scanlon refused to continue the game unless O'Rourke produced the ball, so New York packed up their equipment to leave the grounds. Only the introduction of a new, standard ball allowed play to continue, while commentators speculated whether this chicanery might be responsible for New York's strong offensive showing from the day before.[12] O'Rourke's curious behavior also raises the question of why he would risk getting caught cheating in an exhibition game that did not even count in the official standings. It certainly suggests money was at stake and that some of the players were gambling on the results of the game.

A few players pioneered another trick regarding the ball itself. In the 1880s, the rules called for having just two baseballs for play at a time. As long as the umpire believed a ball was in shape for play, he did not replace it. As the game went along, therefore, these two balls became darker in color, softer, and scuffed as batters hit them and they passed through the dirt and grass during play. The further the ball's condition eroded from its original state, the better for the pitcher because balls that were less white, softer, and scuffed were harder for batters to see, hit for distance, or hit at all. The team at bat would have a distinct advantage if it could convince the umpire it was time to introduce a new ball and toss out an old one. The reverse was true for the team in the field—it would benefit most from keeping the older ball in the game. As a result, in 1888, two International League pitchers, Bob Barr and Pete Wood, tried a new tactic to make sure they got to pitch a well-used ball. When umpires finally decided to throw out an old ball and introduce a new one, they of course preferred the other remaining ball to the brand new one. Therefore, to make sure they were pitching with the older ball, their first pitch with the new ball would "accidentally" fly over the batter's head and either into or entirely over the grandstand. Others began to imitate them, until International League executives instructed their umpires to fine pitchers $25 whenever this took place.[13]

Another example of creative play and bending the rules to New York's advantage occurred early in the championship season of 1885, when the Giants faced off with the Chicago White Stockings. These two teams, the two best in the National League that season, were in the eighth inning of a tie game when New York's catcher, Buck Ewing, intentionally swung at a wild pitch from Chicago's John Clarkson when he had two strikes. Baseball's rules state the batter can attempt to reach first base on a strikeout if the catcher does not catch the pitch cleanly. The defense must throw the batter out at first base to complete the out if this happens. Knowing this, Ewing took his chances that the ball would escape from Chicago's catcher, Sy Sutcliffe, and swung and missed the ball on purpose. It did elude Sutcliffe, Ewing reached base, and later came around to score the winning run of the game. While legal, strictly speaking, Ewing's play clearly perverted the intent of the original rule, and not all baseball observers considered such actions honorable.[14]

The same was true of another questionable strategy for reaching base, this one popularized by Arlie Latham, third baseman for the

St. Louis Browns. In 1886, a sportswriter mentioned the diminutive infielder as the originator of a subtle tactic for reaching base. Latham's technique was to foul away pitches intentionally, just to make the pitcher work harder and eventually throw enough balls that Latham could walk to first. That way, he could avoid the risk of the defense putting him out and reach base safely. Some observers deplored this maneuver as an unmanly bending of the rules, but others approved of Latham's ingenuity and creativity.[15] He also developed a less controversial strategy for securing hits in which he would move his bat into position to bunt the ball, thus causing the infielders to charge in to defend the bunt. At the last moment, however, Latham would pull the bat back and slap at the pitch, swinging with his wrists, attempting to drop the ball just over the heads of the onrushing fielders and score a hit in that manner.[16]

No one, however, not even Billy Taylor, had more tricks and subtleties than Mike Kelly did. New York Giants manager Jim Mutrie once told the story of how, in a game at the Polo Grounds in New York, Kelly was on second base for Chicago when Cap Anson drove the ball into right field for a hit. As Kelly rounded third (observers debated whether he even touched third) Giants right fielder Mike Dorgan uncorked a wild throw to home plate. The ball sailed up the third base line and through an open gate that led under the grandstand. While Giants catcher Tom Deasley and pitcher Tim Keefe raced under the stands to retrieve Dorgan's errant throw, Kelly hustled over and shut the gate, standing in front of it to prevent the ball from coming back onto the field. Anson, meanwhile, circled the bases and scored a run for the White Stockings.[17] Philadelphia Quakers outfielder Jim Fogarty also got credit for performing this manner of interference against Indianapolis in 1888.[18]

Like Hugh Nicol, Kelly had his own version of hiding an extra ball in the outfield. When Kelly joined the Boston Beaneaters and played the outfield at Boston's South End Grounds, if the batter hit a home run over the fence that barely cleared the wall, he would suddenly scramble after the imaginary ball that had "caromed off the top of the wall," grab a ball secreted in his uniform, and fire that ball to teammates to halt the progress of the baserunners.[19] Another of his tactics to defend against the home run while playing the outfield was, if it was late in the game and difficult to see clearly because it was getting dark, he would fake a catch of a home run that traveled over the fence, extract his extra ball from his uniform, and return it to the infield.[20]

Because he often played catcher when not patrolling the outfield, Mike Kelly also perfected a defensive technique as catcher to impede baserunners. One of baseball's oldest plays used to pressure the defense comes when the offense has men on first and third base. The man on first attempts to steal second, and when the catcher throws the ball to second to prevent the stolen base, the man on third breaks for home plate. Kelly's strategy for disrupting this play was, after throwing down to second, to toss his catcher's mask into the baserunner's path about four feet from home plate. Unable to slide for the risk of injury, the baserunner attempting to score from third base had to arrive at home plate standing up after avoiding the mask, leaving Kelly with a split-second of extra time to apply a tag against the runner. A few other catchers learned to copy this trick. Eventually, however, baserunners responded by stomping on Kelly's mask at non-critical times, such as when he tossed it away to chase a foul pop-up, to smash it and make him finish the game without one.[21]

With just one umpire to watch the game, anything went on the base paths when that umpire was watching the action in the field. Baserunners might cut corners and not touch every base, but defenses had a response: interfering with baserunners when they tried to advance. Besides pitchers interfering with a runner on his way to first, if the ball entered the outfield and the action there distracted the umpire's gaze, infielders would slow down baserunners by grabbing belts, tugging shirts, and tripping the runner. Some went a step or two further, even punching, shoulder blocking, or tackling their opponents. The St. Louis Browns, following the example set by their first baseman and captain, Charles Comiskey, were famous for these tactics of rough play. Just one example out of many occurred in an August 1887 game with Cincinnati. When speedy runner Hugh Nicol had a chance to advance a base on a wild throw, Browns shortstop Jack Gleason tackled him to the ground and did his best to apply a chokehold and prevent "Little Nick" from advancing at a key point in the game. Although Nicol did deliver a sharp kick to the shins of Gleason in return, he did not advance an extra base or score a run, and "this garroter's trick robbed Cincinnati of a chance to win."[22]

It was possible to go too far, however. In May of 1888, Indianapolis was playing Chicago when one of the Hoosiers, third baseman Jerry Denny, dove back to second base to avoid a tag by White Stockings second baseman Fred Pfeffer. He arrived safely, and when Pfeffer dropped the throw, Denny proceeded to grab the ball and hurl it into the outfield, advancing himself to third base in the process. When the Chicago outfield returned the ball to third baseman Ned Williamson and he applied a tag to Denny, the umpire declared Denny out. Incredibly, Denny protested the call, but eventually retired to the bench.[23] Although this did not work for Denny, it did for former Louisville outfielder Monk Cline. Playing for Memphis in the Southern League, he snatched the ball away from a fielder and flung it into the outfield to advance a base, just as Denny had done, but in this case, umpire Edward Hengle did not call him out.[24] This demonstrates that having a courageous umpire on hand who was willing to enforce the spirit of the rules, rather than merely their letter, made quite a difference in how frequently the players attempted to cheat.

While these stories might make it appear that nearly every shady maneuver worked, this was not always true. The attitude and perceptiveness of the umpire mattered, and smart ballplayers took the umpire's identity into account when deciding how to cheat. One of the most important decisions that umpires made in this respect was when to call off a game, either because of darkness or rain. With no night baseball and no domed stadiums in the 1880s, this situation lent itself to a great deal of cheating and manipulation because in baseball, the game is official if it lasts for at least five innings. The team ahead after five could claim victory if the umpire deemed conditions unfit for continuing the game because of wetness or darkness. During the 1880s, without Daylight Savings Time, darkness was an important consideration for games, especially early or late in the season. As a result, the team leading after five innings often initiated stalling tactics unimaginable today if it felt the umpire might call off the game soon.

For instance, consider the 1885 game between the New York Metropolitans and their cross-borough rivals from Brooklyn. It was an overcast September day, and in the fourth inning, New York led 4-0 when scattered raindrops started falling. At first, Brooklyn's players complained to umpire John Connelly that the field was unplayable and the game could not continue, thus hoping to avoid a probable defeat by having Connelly call the game before five innings were complete. When Connelly remained unmoved by their entreaties, the Brooklyn players immediately employed various delaying tactics to slow the game and force a cancellation while more rain fell. The key to their filibustering was pitcher Henry Porter, whose "conduct made him the recipient of loud, long, and continued hissing. He wiped the ball with sawdust every time before he delivered it, saying, 'it's wet,' and several times would drop it on the wet grass for the purpose of getting it wet again." It was all for naught, however, because despite some heavy rainfall, Connelly would not cancel the game until after the seventh inning when it was truly pouring.[25]

Cincinnati performed another variation of this maneuver in a July 1888 game against Brooklyn. Brooklyn led 2-0 in the fifth inning when the skies darkened and rain began to fall. At that point the Red Stockings began stalling to get the game rained out before five innings ended. Lee Viau was Cincinnati's pitcher when the mischief began. He retired the first two men of the inning, and then

126

threw a pitch to the backstop because it took more time to retrieve the ball that way. Then the Red Stockings, realizing this was not nearly slow enough to achieve their objective, pulled out all the stops:

> He pitched the ball and it again went into the grand stand, Baldwin again got it and this time threw it away out to Corkhill at center field. Corkhill gazed at the ball and stood like a lump on a log for a few moments. Fennelly then walked lazily out into the field, picked the ball up and threw it over Reilly's head. Reilly made a great splurge for the ball, got it and fired it away over Carpenter's head. As Carpenter picked up the ball and threw it in to Viau, the rain came down in torrents.[26]

The plan worked in a way because umpire John McQuaid had to call off the game at that point. Before doing so, however, he fined Reilly, Carpenter, Viau, and Baldwin twenty-five dollars each for their shenanigans. Outraged, Brooklyn's owner, Charles Byrne, accosted Cincinnati owner Aaron Stern and told him, "Now I do not propose to submit to any further robbery. I insist, even though it cost me my share of the gate receipts, that you at least protect your patrons in giving them back their money or rain checks, since that you robbed them of the opportunity of seeing a game of ball." Stern chose rain checks, and Cincinnati picked up an expensive cancelled game.[27]

Pittsburgh employed a subtle variation of this trick when faced with some rain before a late May game with Indianapolis in 1888. In this case, the team from the Smoky City tried to circumvent the judgment of the umpire altogether. In the 1880s, the home club determined the suitability of its grounds for play before the game started; only after the action commenced did the umpire gain this authority. Pittsburgh management knew this and realized that it did not have many cranks on hand for its game because of the questionable weather. Pittsburgh still had to pay the visitors from

Indianapolis a $150 guarantee for playing the game, however, no matter how few spectators braved Mother Nature's surliness. Therefore, Pittsburgh management decided to take preemptive action and cancel the game. This outraged Indianapolis because the Hoosiers claimed the grounds were quite playable given a bit of sawdust and sand, and when the sun came out during the afternoon and dried up the grounds, they vowed revenge on the Alleghenys for cheating them of their guaranteed share of the gate receipts.[28]

This was not the only time that Pittsburgh management was guilty of shenanigans of this type, either. Just a few days later, in fact, they pulled the same trick on the New York Giants but with an even more infuriating financial sleight of hand. Pittsburgh executive Horace Phillips declared the game was off at about 1:30 in the afternoon but failed to notify New York manager Jim Mutrie of the fact. Mutrie, therefore, brought his men to the grounds at Recreation Park as planned, paying eight dollars for the transportation of his players. Upon arrival, he found there would be no game that day and then paid for transport once again to return his team to its lodgings. The only entity to profit from the fiasco was the omnibus company Mutrie paid to haul his team to the ballpark and back. The president of this company was none other than the same man who also was president of the Pittsburgh Baseball Club.[29]

Mutrie and the Giants returned the favor shortly afterward, however, when the schedule called for Pittsburgh to play at New York's Polo Grounds in early June. Rain had fallen at the Pittsburgh hotel, the Rossmore, most of the day. At 2:30, Phillips telegraphed to the Polo Grounds for instructions of whether to bring his nine to the grounds for the game or not. Mutrie did not answer, and Pittsburgh only received a response when New York owner John Day sent one at 3:55, stating the game was on. Because the game began at 4:00 and the Alleghenys could not reach the ballpark within five minutes, the umpire declared New York the winner by forfeit.[30]

Besides giving the other team misinformation, or no information at all, regarding whether a scheduled game would take place, teams could also try to gain a home field advantage by manipulating the home environment itself. Besides the individual ground rules that were unique to many ballparks in the days before permanent outfield fences were common, teams employed other tactics to get a leg up on the competition. The Philadelphia Athletics, for instance, painted their grandstand white for the 1887 season, believing "the idea that it will injure the players' eyes and affect their play is fallacious. Of course it will affect the men a little at first, but the home team will soon get used to it and as for the visiting players, if they should happen to be affected it will rather inure to the benefit of the home team. See?"[31]

In another case, the Athletics tried to prepare for a series with the St. Louis Browns in 1886 but believed that the aggressive baserunning tactics of the Browns gave the visitors a decided advantage. Seeking to neutralize the Browns' speed, the Athletics responded by spreading loose gravel around second and third base, hoping that the threat of injury from the rocks might deter any base stealing. The strategy failed, however, when the Browns located brooms and swept the gravel away before the game began.[32]

These instances of dishonest play add color to the game of nineteenth century baseball. It is true they made the outcome of games less certain and, in a sense, less honest, but at least they had the relative virtue that any team might employ the tactics, and everyone who played the game knew who the cheaters were and which players they must keep an eye on. Getting quality umpires helped deter shady practices, too. As a result, looking back today, efforts at cheating in 1880s baseball tend to bring a smile to the face of some, while others shake their heads. The game might be a bit less fair, but these antics did not cause observers to question the basic, fundamental honesty of the game, or fear for the safety of the men involved.

We cannot say the same about two other major issues in baseball at the time, gambling and on-field violence. The reader will find a thorough treatment of gambling in the book *Outside the Lines of*

Gilded Age Baseball: Gambling, Umpires, and Racism in 1880s Baseball, but now we must examine violence on the field to conclude our look at the habits of ballplayers in the Gilded Age.

---

[1] "Caught on the Fly," *The Sporting News*, August 9, 1886, 5.

[2] "Notes and Comments," *The Sporting Life*, May 16, 1888, 9.

[3] Nick Young, "For League Umpires," *The Sporting Life*, April 27, 1887, 5.

[4] T. T. T., "Baltimore Bulletin," *The Sporting Life*, August 7, 1889, 2.

[5] Taken from Gaffney's retrosheet page, www.retrosheet.org/boxesetc/G/Pgaffj801.htm, accessed August 21, 2017.

[6] Joe Pritchard, "St. Louis Siftings," *The Sporting Life*, August 7, 1889, 2. "Robbie" was Browns second baseman William "Yank" Robinson.

[7] "Caught on the Fly," *The Sporting News*, August 9, 1886, 5.

[8] F. W. S., "Mr. Kelly of Boston," *The Sporting News*, May 19, 1888, 1.

[9] Circle, "Pittsburg Pencilings," *The Sporting Life*, August 1, 1888, 7.

[10] Daniel Pearson, *Baseball in 1889: Players vs. Owners*, (Bowling Green State University Popular Press, 1993): 13.

[11] Gustav Axelson, *COMMY: The Life Story of Charles A. Comiskey*, (Chicago: Reilly & Lee Co, 1919): 74.

[12] "A Tie Game in Washington," *New York Times*, April 28, 1885, 2.

[13] "Notes and Comments," *The Sporting Life*, May 23, 1888, 9.

[14] "The Chicagos Beaten," *New York Times*, May 16, 1885, 2.

[15] T. T. T., "From Baltimore," *The Sporting Life*, November 10, 1886, 4.

[16] Henry Chadwick, "Chadwick's Chat," *The Sporting Life*, January 26, 1887, 2.

[17] Mugwump, "From the Hub," *The Sporting Life*, March 30, 1887, 3.

[18] "Philadelphia Pointers," *The Sporting Life*, July 11, 1888, 9.

[19] Mugwump, "Hub Happenings," *The Sporting Life*, August 7, 1889, 4.

[20] Pearson, *Baseball in 1889*, 13.

[21] "The Same Tricky Kelly," *The Sporting Life*, October 3, 1888, 1.

[22] Ren Mulford, Jr., "From Cincinnati," *The Sporting Life*, August 17, 1887, 3.

[23] "Notes and Comments" *The Sporting Life*, May 16, 1888, 9.

[24] "Notes and Comments" *The Sporting Life*, June 13, 1888, 10.

[25] "On the Diamond Field," *New York Times*, September 6, 1885, 2.

[26] "Stern and Byrne," *The Sporting News*, July 7, 1888, 7.

[27] Ibid.

[28] "The Hoosiers Charge Phillips With Sharp Practice," *The Sporting News*, June 2, 1888, 1.

[29] Circle, "That Forfeited Game," *The Sporting Life*, June 6, 1888, 1.

[30] "That Forfeited Game," *The Sporting Life*, June 13, 1888, 1.

[31] "Local News," *The Sporting Life*, February 23, 1887, 5.

[32] Nemec, *The Beer and Whiskey League*, 118.

Chapter 6

Violence on the Field

On and off the field, Gilded Age baseball could be quite rough. In his *Historical Baseball Abstract*, no less an observer than Bill James ranked on-field violence as the second worst problem in the game during the 1880s, right below the introduction of segregation and above such things as arguments with management, frequent player movement, and alcoholism. By the 1890s, on-field violence rated first in James' eyes, surpassing even racial segregation as baseball's greatest sin.[1] While I believe James underrated the issue of drinking, violent behavior no doubt was a discredit to many players and something that both team management and the union of National League players, the Brotherhood of Professional Baseball Players, tried to counteract in the eyes of the public.

Both groups had a lot of counteracting to do. Cleveland sportswriter F. H. Brunell wrote that baseball needed "to squelch the idea held by the general public that a ball player is a tough, unfit for decent society, a creature of people of sporting tastes to be tolerated in his public capacity because of his peculiar talents, but not fit for society other than his own and his immediate admirers." Brunell saw hope, however, and believed the Brotherhood might play an important role in elevating the moral stature of the game, writing, "There has been a moral growth among the ball players of the last six years. . . . The Brotherhood can help it, and the Brotherhood should, and should also extend its arms as far as possible. This will be an influence that the public cannot resist—that of merit."[2]

Violence took many forms and happened at all levels of the game. Sometimes, players got rough in their efforts to hold back the opposition, considering physical play to be part of the game. St. Louis Browns center fielder Curt Welch was one such player. In the fifth inning of a game on June 9, 1887, an opponent, Philadelphia Athletics pitcher Gus Weyhing, struck the ball and scampered towards second base for a double. Welch ran all the way to second base from his position in center field and upon arriving at the infield, "struck Weyhing with his clinched fist in order to prevent the latter from making second." The American Association fined him forty-five dollars for this and various other offenses perpetrated that day.[3]

Other Browns played just as dirty. Second baseman Yank Robinson had a habit of punching baserunners in the gut when they rounded second base to deprive them of their wind, if he thought that some other event on the field had distracted the umpire's eyes.[4] Curt Welch was also among the group of players with a habit of leaning over home plate to let pitches hit him while at bat. The goal, of course, was a free trip to first base for taking a hit by pitch. Baseball rules, even then, stated that a batter should try to evade a pitched ball rather than let the ball hit him on purpose, but different umpires enforced this rule with different degrees of stringency. Statistics corroborate Welch's reputation, too. He led the American Association in times hit by the pitch in three seasons. As Joe Pritchard put it, "He would stop any kind of a ball with his ribs in order to gain the initial bag."[5] The umpire had the power to deny the batter a free base in this instance, but because this was a judgment call, it encouraged rowdy arguments and more kicking by either the batter or pitcher, depending on which way the umpire called the play.[6]

Contributing to Welch's ungentlemanly style was his fondness for liquor. According to contemporaries, he could drink almost any amount and not miss a beat while playing, either at bat or in the field. As one writer put it,

> He stands unrivaled as an outfielder. He makes plays that other outfielders cannot touch with such little effort that the plays lose half of their effect as they look to be easy. What makes his great work all the more remarkable is the fact that he does not take care of himself. It is a fact that Welch very frequently comes on the ball field almost stupid from his excess in liquor, with a load on that would put most men to bed. In spite of his drunkenness he will make almost impossible catches, hit the ball hard and run bases in grand style. He is the only ball player who can drink and play good ball.[7]

Nor was Welch especially picky about when he imbibed. A saloon, pool hall, or bar was best, certainly, but not a requirement. Anywhere would do: "Welch nearly threw away his career in his rookie year at Toledo by swilling beer whenever there was a break in action—an argument with an umpire or a conference in the pitcher's box—from a stash he hid behind a loose board in the outfield fence at the Blue Stockings park."[8]

Welch did not learn his lesson from his healthy fine for his assault on Weyhing. Just six days later, in Baltimore, he did a similar thing to Orioles player Bill Greenwood, only this time Welch was the baserunner. The "game between the Orioles and the Browns was truncated by a crowd riot after Welch smashed into Baltimore second baseman Bill Greenwood on a steal attempt. Barnie and Oyster Burns . . . both rushed onto the field in street clothes to assail Welch and several spectators exhorted a policeman to arrest the Browns star for assault." The police did arrest Welch, and the

Browns had to pay $200 to bail him out of jail to play the next day. This time, it is possible that Welch went too far, even for the Browns. A short time later Tip O'Neill, one of the largest men on the team, "accidentally" lost control of his bat during a swing while Welch was in the on-deck circle. The bat flew towards Welch and struck him in the face. This seems to have been a message from his teammates that enough was enough.[9]

Although he was the aggrieved party in St. Louis in 1887, Weyhing did not necessarily mind the rough and tumble. Just two months later, he was involved in another ruckus. He drove the ball into the outfield at the home grounds of the New York Metropolitans on Staten Island, whereupon he reached third base. The umpire ordered him back to second, claiming that the ground rules for the park dictated a double for any ball hit in that location. Weyhing refused to retreat, "the players and umpire were soon mixed up in an excited mass," and eventually Umpire Sullivan awarded the game to New York by forfeit when he could not restore order.[10] In spite of his willingness to risk injury in physical confrontations, Weyhing had a long career in major league baseball and, true to the reputation the stories above seem to give him, he is easily the all-time leader among pitchers in hitting batters with pitches. He plunked 277 men in his career, far outdistancing the second-place pitcher, Chick Fraser. In fact, in his first two seasons, Weyhing hit 79 men with pitches, nearly one per game.

The roughhouse tactics employed by Welch and Robinson were, by many accounts, typical of the entire St. Louis Browns organization. Another characteristic episode occurred in 1885, when the Browns had the bases loaded in a close game. On a ground ball to the shortstop, the shortstop threw home, and Browns baserunner Bill Gleason collided with the catcher at home plate and knocked him to the ground, dislodging the ball in the process. He continued wrestling with the catcher, Jack O'Brien, until both other baserunners and the batter had circled the bases and scored. Because the incident took place at the Browns' home grounds of Sportsman's

Park, "the umpire would have declared all hands out, but that he valued his life too highly."[11]

Although he did not become a full-time major league player until joining the Browns in 1888, Tommy McCarthy was already a full-time thug in the eyes of many contemporaries. As a result, he had no trouble fitting in with his new mates in the Mound City. Early in that season, McCarthy and John Reilly of Cincinnati earned reputations for continually spiking fielders as they slid into bases, in the hope of distracting them from catching the ball or applying a tag. (It is interesting to see Reilly accused of this tactic, considering that in the off-season, he would walk alone in the forest and make artistic sketches of woodland scenes, but competition can bring out both the best and worst in people.[12]) When attempting to spike someone, as the runner slides into a base, he raises one foot and kicks at the fielder with his spiked shoe, usually striking for the shin. While this violent practice helped McCarthy in the short run, it was dangerous if done repeatedly because fielders had ways to strike back. One player explained, "If McCarthy, Reilly, or any other dirty ball player ever spikes me intentionally, I will signal my catcher to throw the ball high to me the very next time that player starts to come my way, and if I don't jump high into the air and bring my spikes down squarely on him and spike him so badly that he won't play a month after that my name ain't -----."[13]

McCarthy also gives us an example of how, under the right (or wrong) circumstances, fans might be victims of player violence, as well. During his initial campaign in 1888, when St. Louis visited Cincinnati for a series of games, outfielder McCarthy tried to peg a Cincinnati fan with the ball during a game. The batter, Kid Baldwin, hit the ball into the outfield crowd and while McCarthy retrieved it, one of the spectators began taunting him. Rather than return the ball to the infield to halt Baldwin's progress, however, McCarthy attempted to bean the fan instead. He missed, and Baldwin circled the bases before anyone could retrieve the ball. This behavior demonstrated a pattern on McCarthy's part; earlier that year he attempted to do the same to umpire Bob Ferguson when Ferguson's call did not go his way.[14]

A game need not even happen during the championship season to provoke fights and rows. Another example of on-field violence occurred during an exhibition match between the New York Metropolitans and the minor league Newark team just prior to the 1886 season. Two players, Tom Foster of the Metropolitans and Tom "Oyster" Burns (not the same Tom Burns as the man who played third base for the Chicago White Stockings that same year and who had no shellfish-based nickname) of Newark engaged in fisticuffs following a raft of verbal abuse directed from Burns toward Foster. The dispute arose over the umpiring performance of former major league player Dave Pierson, whom both teams accused of inconsistency in his interpretation of the rules. At one point, Pierson called a balk on Newark pitcher John "Phenomenal" Smith, and when Burns protested and Foster stood up for Pierson's call, Burns became infuriated and struck the Metropolitan second baseman: "This was the signal for the crowd to take part in the row. Men and boys left their seats, and in an instant all was confusion. . . . While the trouble was at its height, one man rushed out on the field with a revolver in his hand. Some of his friends interfered, and before he could do any damage he was disarmed."[15] Eventually, law enforcement restored order, herding the 300-400 brawling spectators off the grounds. Unsurprisingly, New York manager Jim Gifford pulled his club off the field, and shortly thereafter, American Association Chairman Charles Byrne instructed Association teams to boycott all further games with Newark while Burns remained a member of the club.[16]

While some blamed Burns for inciting the crowd to riot, others had a different story. Some defended the Newark infielder, with *The Sporting Life* offering "the Washington papers generally sympathize with Burns, and rejoice at the thrashing he gave Foster, of the Mets, who is described as a good player but quarrelsome." Burns asked Newark for his release as his penalty for his volatile behavior, but the team rejected his request. He ended up on the blacklist instead, although he later cleared his name. That same week, some New York fans attempted to avenge their man, Foster, by assaulting Burns on the streets. Burns required a police escort to a safe house for protection.[17] Although best known as an outfielder, by 1887 he was playing shortstop for Billy Barnie in Baltimore, where he produced several solid seasons as a hitter but never quite shook his temper. At least he admitted he had a problem: "Tom admits having the hottest kind of a temper which is easily ruffled, but claims that no serious troubles need ever be apprehended on that score if he is properly dealt with. What he asks, he says, are respectful demands and he will readily comply with them."[18]

The story of Burns and Foster demonstrates that players sometimes instigated fights with each other. Tommy McCarthy demonstrated that they instigated the occasional fight with fans as well. McCarthy had a bit of company in these efforts, however. In an 1886 exhibition game in St. Louis, Maroons pitcher Al Bauer nearly made a heckling fan into a landscaping tool: "Bauer, of the Maroons, is perhaps the most muscular ball-player in the profession. During one of the recent games at Sportsman's Park, someone in the crowd where Bauer was standing made an insulting remark about the Maroons, and Bauer almost made a hole in the fence with him."[19]

It seems like this penchant for aggressiveness would have served Bauer well when he ended his mediocre pitching career ("because his exertions caused his arm to lose its cunning"[20]) and became an American Association umpire before the 1887 season, considering all the abuse that baseball's officials took from players and cranks, but it appears he was just as mediocre an umpire as he was a pitcher, at least initially. Just two weeks into the 1887 season, Bauer had already made enemies of St. Louis owner Chris Von der Ahe and Louisville's Zack Phelps, who alleged they had "suffered as the result of his work against them in all games in which he has officiated thus far," and these men tried to engineer Bauer's dismissal because "he was so deficient in the necessary qualifications of a fair and correct interpretation of the rules as to make it a hardship and a wrong to compel clubs to play under him."[21] A Louisville sportswriter at one of the games agreed that Bauer's work had not given satisfaction but that his lack of judgment showed no favoritism and that players for St. Louis, especially first baseman Charlie Comiskey and second baseman Yank Robinson, had kicked so badly that they delayed the game with their whining over Bauer's decisions. Robinson also had the nerve to cut twenty feet in front of third base while trying to score on one hit, and this almost produced a fight with Louisville catcher John Kerins when Bauer failed to notice the subterfuge.[22] Bauer resigned from the American Association's umpiring staff on May 6.[23] Following his failure in the Association, he signed on in the Ohio League that same year and improved his work to the point that the desperate Association gave him another chance in August when Ted Sullivan threw in the towel in disgust over his treatment.[24]

Apparently, Bauer spent his time in the Ohio League productively because "Al Bauer made his reappearance as an American Association umpire here yesterday and there wasn't a chirp of dissatisfaction from either audience or players. The game was quickly played—it required one hour and eighteen minutes to finish it—and was the shortest on the home grounds this year." Even though each team put "four or five players on the coach line at once" so the players could whine about favoritism and poor calls, "it was a game in which the coacher had little to do," and Bauer sailed through the game "without hearing a word of protest from either side." Cincinnati manager Gus Schmelz even went so far as to say, "His work to-day has not been excelled this season!"[25] Bauer continued earning praise in the environment of the minor leagues. Working for the Tri-State League in 1888, one Columbus writer praised his performance by writing, "He is one of the fairest and best posted umpires in the business. He is not a home umpire. He plays no favorites, and any club that wins a game over which he presides does so upon the merits of their superiority. He is absolutely fearless, and will not be bulldozed. Sober and reliable, a gentleman at all times."[26]

Given how much ballplayers hated umpires, it is a wonder fights between the two groups did not happen more frequently, especially against umpires less physically imposing than Al Bauer or Bob Ferguson. A few notable incidents took place, however. One of the worst cases of fighting between a player and umpire at the major league level took place at the end of the 1889 campaign. In a game between Cleveland and Boston, Beaneaters captain Mike Kelly arrived at the grounds intoxicated, forcing manager Jim Hart to relegate the star player to the bench for the day. After an unexceptional call went against his men, Kelly rushed the field to give the umpire, John McQuaid, a piece of his mind. Just as Kelly drew back his arm to strike a blow, teammates Charlie Bennett and John Clarkson tried to restrain him. While Kelly pushed them away, McQuaid had just enough time to call for police protection so that when Kelly made another rush at him, the officers took the King by the throat and escorted him from the grounds.[27]

Kansas City Cowboys catcher Charlie Hoover got himself into hot water for reasons with which McCarthy and Bauer were familiar late in the 1889 season. When some members of the home crowd started giving him grief for poor catching in an October 3 game, Hoover let a pitch get to the backstop on purpose. Instead of retrieving the ball, however, "the catcher pulled off his gloves, threw down his chest protector and climbed over into the seats. He had blood in his eye and was looking for the man who had presumed to guy him. The individual who did the yelling was just at this time the quietest man on the grounds." Mortified at such behavior, Cowboy management removed Hoover from the game after the inning concluded (rules prevented mid-inning substitutions at the time, except for cases of injury) and decided to suspend him for the remainder of the season. After his team relieved him of duty, Hoover left the bench to drink away his frustration in a nearby saloon.[28]

Even though it looked very bad when a player lost his composure and went after a spectator, the behavior of the spectators often was such that it was hard to blame the players for wanting to strike back. A sarcastic article written for *The Sporting Life* in 1886 gives readers an idea of the ungentlemanly behavior of some spectators: "When there is a high wind smoke cigars with broken wrappers. Those next to you will have their interest in the game greatly increased if their eyes are filled with tobacco ashes." In addition, the writer advised sarcastically, "the managers are always pleased to have their attention called to the weak points of the nine. It isn't to be supposed that the gentlemen who have thousands of dollars at risk would notice defects in the players as soon as the spectator." Finally:

Don't be so credulous as to believe the umpire is selected because of his knowledge of the game. There was never known a base ball audience that couldn't tell a pitched ball better than he. One reason for this is because the umpire stands too near the home plate and almost in a direct line with the batsman and pitcher. It is reasonable to suppose that the spectators opposite the second and third bases are far more competent to detect pitchers' errors than a person in the position described.[29]

O. P. Caylor also noticed that spectators, no matter where they sat, always believed they knew better than the umpire did. He sarcastically suggested, therefore, that the umpire call the game from a similarly distant point: "Maybe a balloon anchored several hundred feet above the diamond would be a handy place for him. Then he would be out of reach of beer glasses, and if he made a mistake he could cut the cables and sail away out of danger, thus doing away with a strong police escort."[30] Detroit's president in 1886, Marsh, poked fun at fans' behavior, too: "I've got an idea. I am going to have some cards printed. On one set I will have the reasons why our club did not win the last game; on another, the condition of all our pitchers, and on another, the reasons why Brouthers doesn't knock the cover off the ball every time he comes to bat. . . . It will give me a rest, and perhaps I can recuperate before the scheme wears out."[31]

Competition has a strange way of bringing out a side of ballplayers, and people generally, that rarely appears during everyday activities. This was certainly true of pitcher Tony Mullane. Off the field, Mullane courted a reputation as a dude or dandy. Among his nicknames was "the Count of Macaroni" because macaroni was an expression for someone attempting a stylish appearance.[32] Mullane was also a very skilled pitcher, known on the field as "the Apollo of the Box," whose contract hijinks were legion. However, Mullane, despite his off-field reputation, was not averse to brawling when he felt so inclined. In particular, he had great deal of bad blood toward second baseman Sam Barkley, who once threw his bat at the pitcher during an exhibition game. Mullane, while pitching for Cincinnati, also got into fisticuffs with Cleveland utility player Bob Gilks after an exhibition game in 1889. During the game, Gilks accused Mullane of trying to hit him with pitches intentionally, knowing that Mullane had a reputation for trying to intimidate batters who could hit his curveball, and they exchanged words. After the game, Mullane entered Cleveland's dressing room, stating he wanted to explain himself to his opponent. Gilks, not feeling conciliatory, grabbed a bat and feinted at Mullane, whereupon the Count of Macaroni grappled Gilks and tossed him to the floor, landing several blows before teammates and police separated the two.[33]

Just as Frank Brunell stated in his quote at the beginning of this chapter, one of the biggest problems with violence on the field was that it discouraged fans from coming to the ballpark. True, rowdy play and constant brawls might attract a few spectators, much like fighting in hockey or car crashes in auto racing entice a few people to watch such sports today, but for the most part, fans wanted to see baseball and appreciate the action that was part of the game. Fans cared about seeing hard hits, aggressive baserunning, diving stops in the field, and crafty pitching. If, collectively, they decided that baseball players were hoodlums who just happened to be lucky and have a bit of athletic ability, they might stay home, and no professional sports league can succeed without support from spectators. That is part of the reason why managers and team owners feared alcohol so much—in addition to making players perform poorly, it contributed to undesirable things on the field like fights and disputes.

Given the stake that team managers had in making sure that games ran smoothly and professionally, then, we might expect that they would try to set an example for their men and avoid rows and violent arguments themselves. Surprisingly, however, this did not always happen. In an 1887 exhibition game against Des Moines, Mobile's manager, named Kelly, entered the stands to do battle with a spectator applauding the Des Moines nine too vigorously: "A row followed and the result was that a meeting was called that night at which Manager Kelly was suspended." In addition to a fine, as further disciplinary action, Mobile cautioned Kelly, "under no provocation whatever, should he give way to his temper, under penalty of dismissal."[34]

Besides taking on unruly or boisterous fans, managers might also brawl with members of their own nine. That is what nearly happened in Kansas City in 1888, when manager Dave Rowe got into the face of right fielder Jim McTammany after McTammany allowed a ball to get past him in that day's game. Rowe threatened his own player, according to witnesses, telling McTammany, "If it had not been that so many people were in the grand stand this afternoon, I would have left my place, gone out into the field to you and smashed your jaw, for allowing that grounder to pass you." Taken aback, McTammany protested that his effort was up to par and he was trying his best. His manager replied, "No, you ain't. You are playing lazy ball, and if you let any more ground hits get away from you, I repeat, I'll smash your face." Unable to take any more,

McTammany challenged his manager to make good on his threat on the spot, promising to pay him back with interest for any damage sustained. Separated by other players, the men did not come to blows, but the intensity of the exchange was a lamentable aspect of baseball in this era.[35]

Even rival managers sometimes got into the act, but most of the action was between the competitors on the field. When the Baltimore Orioles traveled to Brooklyn to open the 1889 season, the Orioles displayed both new uniforms and a surly disposition. One of their catchers, a journeyman named Pop Tate, collared Brooklyn's Darby O'Brien when O'Brien threatened to escape a rundown between third and home. Tate dragged O'Brien to the ground, whereupon third baseman Billy Shindle tagged him. The umpire declared O'Brien out, the Brooklyn crowd erupted in protest, and the two clubs exchanged threats.[36] The disturbance caused by hundreds of fans storming the field in protest was so great that the Bridegrooms took the extreme measure of installing a barbed wire fence to separate players and spectators at Ridgewood Park after this fracas.[37]

Some men behaved in such an obnoxious manner that they positively invited retribution in some form. These players, with their constant kicking and willingness to run their mouths too freely, made plenty of enemies. Foremost among such players was "the Freshest Man on Earth," Arlie Latham of the St. Louis Browns. While people also called Latham "the Dude" for his colorful personality and flashy wardrobe, the "fresh" part of his nickname reflected his tendency to speak too provocatively toward opponents: "Latham's coaching methods and his free tongue may be nuts for spectators, but they make him lots of enemies in the profession. The boys have to be careful about scrapping during the playing season, but there is no law against it after the season closes. For this period Latham has no less than twenty fights to settle, five of which are with Robinson, of his own team."[38] Following the 1886 World Series with the Chicago White Stockings, the major Chicago papers lambasted Latham and his jumbled utterings. The *Times* remarked that Latham "made an antiquated idiot out of himself in a vain attempt to rattle the veteran players of the Chicago team," while the *Daily Inter Ocean* deplored "the disgusting mouthings of the clown Latham. There was a universal sentiment of disgust expressed by the crowd that left the ball park at the close of the game at this hoodlum's obscene talk on the ball field." Finally, the *Daily Tribune* stated that one contest was

> chiefly remarkable for the coaching of Latham, a sawed-off Brown, with a voice that would put to shame the most ambitious fog-siren on the lakes. His incessant howling, a meaningless jumble of catch phrases, was funny for about fifteen minutes. Then it grew tiresome, and before the fourth inning he was universally conceded to be the worst nuisance ever inflicted upon a Chicago audience.[39]

Latham's energy and wit was such that, along with another of baseball's most charismatic performers, Mike Kelly, he sometimes performed on stage during the winter months to supplement his income and keep himself occupied.[40] He admitted to having no acting experience at all and, furthermore, to having no idea what he was doing on stage, telling an interviewer, "I just simply accepted the proposition that was made to me last summer and went in on my gall. . . . You see I don't exactly know my part yet. In fact I haven't any part. I just come on and say what I please. It's generally different every time. A part was written for me but I didn't have time to study it."[41] Interestingly, outfielder Emmett Seery tried his hand at being a thespian as well, which seems a strange choice for a man with somewhat of an intellectual reputation for his ability as a chess player.[42] Seery, however, did sing the part of the Assessor in the play *Chimes of Normandy* during the winter of 1888-1889.[43]

Because of baseball's competitive nature, it is no surprise that teammates squared off at times. In Pittsburgh, first baseman Otto

Shomberg (or Schomberg) got into a row with catcher Fred Carroll when Schomberg started rumors that Carroll had it out for him. When the rumors got back to Carroll, he went hunting for the first baseman: "He found him and accused him of carrying tales. This Shomberg denied, and Carroll after applying some language more forcible than polite, hit him. Shomberg immediately retaliated and witnesses say was getting the best of the bout when separated by friends." Later, the two men shook hands and smoothed over their differences, although not before the club fined Carroll fifty dollars for his violent outburst.[44] The team traded Schomberg after the 1886 season, possibly so that the situation with Carroll could not escalate any further.

Another example emerged in Boston in 1888. There, outfielder Joe Hornung and shortstop Sam Wise made each other's enemies list when Wise initiated several fictitious stories meant to discredit the team's left fielder. It appears Wise even paid a visit to Hornung's home, intending to disrupt his marriage and anger his wife, but the woman chased Wise from her home with a carving knife.[45]

Rough tactics were, on occasion, so blatant that one wonders why players even tried them. For instance, consider the May 1889 series in which Indianapolis faced Cleveland, and the actions of the Hoosiers ran the gamut from dumb to imbecile. In one game the umpire ruled Hoosier third baseman Jerry Denny out for baserunner interference. Twice. Meanwhile, catcher Con Daily took up the Mike Kelly practice of tossing his catcher's mask down along the third base line so that runners heading home could not slide without injuring themselves. To top things off, in another game, Daily hit a weak ground ball to the infield with a runner at second base. Angry at his ineffective hit but determined he would reach base anyway, rather than dropping his bat at home plate, he carried it with him down the first base line, finally throwing it at Cleveland first baseman Jay Faatz just as Faatz was about to receive the throw at first base. The umpire let Daily off easy for this violent act, calling him out and mulcting him a paltry ten dollars. It seems only fair that the same game ended when Cleveland fooled a Hoosier baserunner, Jumbo Shoeneck, with the hidden ball trick, which is literally the oldest trick in baseball and works roughly once per decade.[46]

Sadly, in 1885 a dark incident brought home the risks of all the rough play. The Southern League's Atlanta team had a first baseman named Louis Henke. Much bad blood existed between Henke's team and the Nashville nine, and in the August 14 game between the two cities, both sides did everything possible to thwart the efforts of the opponent. In that fateful game, Henke drove a ball into the outfield and ran toward first base with the intent of heading to second. Before he could, however, the Nashville first baseman cut off his path to the base and "assumed a position to meet him, and standing with bent knee, Henke ran against him with tremendous force. He rose, staggered, and fell." Louis Henke died from internal injuries at 5:30 p.m. the next day.[47]

Nor was this the only baseball fatality due to rough play on the field. In 1888, *The Sporting Life* wrote, "spikings are of common occurrence, far more than the public has any idea of, and it is really a matter of wonder that fatalities are not more frequent. Any and every player who suffers from the spikes is liable to meet the fate of the Newark second baseman Simmons, as the danger of blood poisoning is always present, contingent upon the injured man's physical condition or improper treatment of the wound." Because of the death of Simmons, considered among the most promising players in the Central League, the paper advocated the interesting innovation of allowing baserunners to overrun all bases without fear of the fielder putting them out, rather than just first base, putting an end to the need for sliding altogether except for close plays at home plate. It concluded, "It is bad enough to have many valuable players crippled each season without in addition sacrificing their lives to the Moloch of base sliding."[48]

While not quite so dark as seeing ballplayers die on the field or sustain injury, the language used by players toward other players, fans, and umpires was violent, as well. Although the Baltimore

Orioles teams of the National League in the 1890s gained the greatest renown for this, historically speaking, and took the practice to extremes, they had predecessors from whom they drew inspiration. Cap Anson's Chicago teams of the 1880s perfected the art of kicking, and as mentioned earlier, Charlie Comiskey in St. Louis was no slouch when it came to bulldozing opponents and umpires. Some owners liked this because they believed that fans liked it and would pay to see it, although other owners did not, fearing it would hurt baseball's popularity among the spectators, especially female ones.

Trying to halt the verbal assault on fans' ears, the Southern League attempted strong measures against some of its most unrepentant sinners in 1886. Shortstop Marr Phillips, who had played in the majors the prior season with both Detroit and Pittsburgh, nearly had to plead his case to Atlanta's authorities: "Marr Phillips, Charleston's short stop, was arrested at Atlanta last week for profanity upon the ball field and hauled before the chief of police. At the request of the Atlanta Club directors he was discharged and thus saved an appearance in the police court."[49] Curt Welch of the St. Louis Browns was another player known for his profanity: "Welch? There is one thing certain and that is *The Sporting Life* would not publish the talk he indulged in out in center field last Friday, and if he ever sent it to you by mail, he would be liable to indictment by a United States Grand Jury for violating the postal laws."[50]

Despite the occasional distasteful episode on the field, the greatest threat that violence, verbal or physical, posed to the game was the potential damage to baseball's reputation. Every time someone did something violent, and the press found out about it and published the story, the risk people would consider all the players guilty by association increased. This could also hurt management; if the public believed that baseball nines were simply a collection of uncouth hooligans, people might well stay away from the park and spend their money elsewhere. This could even hold true for former players. In February of 1888, for instance, old-time player Dickie Flowers, who once performed for the Troy Haymakers and Philadelphia Athletics back in the National Association days, entered a Philadelphia barroom and engaged in a "playful struggle" with the barkeep, Peter Whalen. He ended up stabbing Whalen in his abdomen, and Whalen died four days later. While a coroner's jury found Flowers innocent of murder, ruling the death accidental, incidents such as this certainly did not improve the reputation of ball players among the sporting pubic.[51]

Ed Beatin, a pitcher with the Detroit Wolverines, also gave his associates reason to fear for their good names. In April of 1888, Beatin attempted to seduce Miss Annie Merkel, of Trexlertown, Pennsylvania, and Miss Merkel retaliated by pressing charges against him. Merkel worked at the Eagle Hotel in Allentown where Beatin had stayed for a time. It took until August for the law to catch up with Beatin, but once it did, he spent two days in jail before settling the case and paying $400 in damages.[52]

When it came to trouble involving young women, worse by far was the case of John Glenn. Like Flowers, Glenn entered major league baseball in the National Association in 1871, lasting long enough to play two National League seasons with the Chicago White Stockings in 1876 and 1877. In the 1880s, Glenn spent time in New York's state prison for assaulting women, including his own niece. He was out of prison by 1887, but, apparently, he had not reformed his ways. In that year he shot at, but missed, a carriage driver while drunk. Then, in November of 1888, he assaulted another person, a nine-year-old girl: "When he was taken to the police court a mob made an attempt to lynch him. The police endeavored to protect him, and in the scuffle that ensued Glenn was accidentally shot in the head by a policeman." He did not die on the spot, but the police moved him to his brother's house for an attempt at recuperation: "If Glenn survives he will most assuredly be lynched. . . . Had he not been shot yesterday the mob would have succeeded in getting him away from the policemen and would have hanged him to the nearest lamp-post." Mob action turned out to be unnecessary, however, because Glenn died from the gunshot two days later, on November 10.[53] Few missed him, it seems, with one writer stating, "Glenn, who was addicted to drink, is one of the very few professionals who have disgraced themselves by criminal conduct. At Sandy Hill, where he resided of late years, not an expression of sympathy for the dead man could be heard. The police officer who accidentally shot him was conceded to be blameless."[54]

With so much on the line in terms of public reputation, teams went to varying lengths to keep their men out of trouble. The precautions teams took against alcohol were many. When Columbus regained major league status and joined the American Association for 1889, its management even drew up a code of conduct for the players.

1 – Players are expected to be gentlemen at all times.

2 – While in Columbus report at grounds daily, except Sunday, at 10 a.m. and 2 p.m., unless excused by captain or manager.

3 – Retire at 11:30 p.m.

4 – No drinking of intoxicants will be allowed at any time.

5 – Players are cautioned against associating with harlots and gamblers.

6 – Avoid pool rooms and saloons.

7 – While in the field the captain has charge of the team, and his authority is not to be questioned at any time.

8 – No finding fault with another player's work will be allowed. If you have any grievance go to the manager.

9 – Players are expected to keep themselves in proper moral and physical condition.

Any breach of these rules resulted in a $10 fine, except for the no-drinking clause, which carried a $50 fine for the first offence and a $100 penalty plus suspension for the second.[55]

In the end, the issue of violence in baseball is important for the same reasons that alcohol abuse, umpire abuse, gambling, dishonesty, and physical fitness were important. All these issues were about improving baseball's image and presenting spectators with a better product for their entertainment half-dollar. Negative incidents involving any of these vices threatened to dampen public enthusiasm for a sport growing in popularity and profitability. No one connected to the game wanted to see those things injured or disrupted, especially the owners who had invested sizable sums in baseball.

Beyond that, the violence injured scores of people, and even killed a handful of them. The reasons people became so angry over the outcome of games were many: pride in their team, preserving their reputation, retaliating against provocations, the intoxicating effect of alcohol, and betting on the outcome of the games, just to name a few. Still, it is hard to justify all the violence. Players often got away with it for the same reasons they could cheat so routinely, that being the absence of a second umpire to help watch everything going on. Yet, fighting did the game no credit then, just as such events do sporting events no credit when they happen today. The wiser players and owners realized this and did their best to curtail it but if this chapter proves anything, it is that baseball still had a long way to go on this front when the 1880s came to an end.

---

[1] James, *The New Bill James Historical Baseball Abstract*, 45, 63.
[2] F. H. Brunell, "From Cleveland," *The Sporting Life*, February 23, 1887, 4.
[3] "Notes of the Game," *New York Times*, June 10, 1887, 2.
[4] "Notes and Comments," *The Sporting Life*, April 27, 1887, 11.
[5] Joe Pritchard, "St. Louis Siftings," *The Sporting Life*, December 5, 1888, 5.
[6] F. H. Brunell, "From Cleveland," *The Sporting Life*, August 31, 1887, 4.
[7] "Philadelphia Pointers," *The Sporting Life*, May 22, 1889, 4.

[8] Nemec, *The Beer and Whiskey League*, 98.

[9] Nemec, *The Beer and Whiskey League*, 138-139.

[10] "Broke Up in a Rumpus," *New York Times*, August 13, 1887, 2.

[11] "Notes and Comments," *The Sporting Life*, May 16, 1888, 9.

[12] Ren Mulford, Jr., "Cincinnati Chips," *The Sporting Life*, November 21, 1888, 3.

[13] "Dirty Ball Playing," *The Sporting Life*, June 6, 1888, 1.

[14] "Notes and Comments" *The Sporting Life*, October 24, 1888, 2.

[15] "Almost a Riot on the Field," *New York Times*, April 9, 1886, 8.

[16] "Notes and Comments," *The Sporting Life*, April 14, 1886, 5; Metropolitan Eyewitness, "The Row at Newark," *The Sporting Life*, April 21, 1886, 1.

[17] "Notes and Comments," *The Sporting Life*, April 21, 1886, 5.

[18] T. T. T., "Baltimore Bulletin," *The Sporting Life*, March 7, 1888, 4.

[19] "Notes and Comments," *The Sporting Life*, April 21, 1886, 5. The author approves of these characterizations of his namesake's physique. Bauer's official measurements were 5'9", 190 pounds.

[20] F. W. Arnold, "Columbus Chatter," *The Sporting Life*, March 27, 1889, 7. Arnold was also the sports editor for the *Columbus Dispatch*.

[21] "Umpire Bauer's Goose Cooked," *The Sporting Life*, April 27, 1887, 1.

[22] X. X. X., "From the Falls City," *The Sporting Life*, April 27, 1887, 5.

[23] "Umpire Bauer Resigns," *The Sporting News*, May 7, 1887, 1.

[24] "Notes and Comments," *The Sporting Life*, August 24, 1887, 5.

[25] Ren Mulford, Jr., "From Cincinnati," *The Sporting Life*, August 31, 1887, 3.

[26] Patrol, "Columbus Chatter," *The Sporting Life*, January 9, 1889, 4.

[27] Commodore, "Cleveland Excited," *The Sporting Life*, October 9, 1889, 6.

[28] Home Run, "Hoover Had a Jag," *The Sporting News*, October 5, 1889, 2.

[29] "A Few Pointers for the Benefit of Spectators at Base Ball Matches," *The Sporting Life*, April 28, 1886, 1.

[30] O. P. Caylor, "Caylor's Comment," *The Sporting Life*, August 21, 1889, 3.

[31] "Notes and Comments," *The Sporting Life*, August 25, 1886, 5.

[32] Now the reader understands the meaning of the tune "Yankee Doodle."

[33] "Tony Mullane as a Slugger," *Chicago Daily Tribune*, April 10, 1889, 5; F. H. Brunell, "Brunell's Budget," *The Sporting Life*, April 17, 1889, 3. Mullane's different nicknames are longer than most nicknames, the 1880s being a time when four- and five-word nicknames appeared relatively frequently.

[34] Jack Brennen, "A Pretty Mess at Mobile," *The Sporting News*, March 12, 1887, 1.

[35] R. W. B., "A Pleasant Episode," *The Sporting Life*, June 20, 1888, 1.

[36] J. F. Donnelly, "Brooklyn Brevities," *The Sporting Life*, May 8, 1889, 3.

[37] "Notes and Comments," *The Sporting Life*, May 15, 1889, 4.

[38] "Notes and Comments," *The Sporting Life*, August 25, 1886, 5.

[39] "Latham's Coaching," *The Sporting Life*, November 3, 1886, 5.

[40] J. A., "Louisville Laconics," *The Sporting Life*, November 21, 1888, 4.

[41] F. K. W., "Cincinnati Chaff," *The Sporting News*, November 24, 1888, 4.

[42] "Seery Turns Actor," *The Sporting News*, November 24, 1888, 1.

[43] "Notes and Comments," *The Sporting Life*, December 5, 1888, 2.

[44] Natural Gas, "From the Smoky City," *The Sporting Life*, August 18, 1886, 4.

[45] "Hornung and Wise," *The Sporting News*, February 25, 1888, 1.

[46] F. H. Brunell, "The 'Spiders,'" *The Sporting Life*, May 22, 1889, 5.

[47] "Killed on the Ball Field," *New York Times*, August 16, 1885, 1.

[48] No title, *The Sporting Life*, December 19, 1888, 2; "The Primary Cause of a Well-Known Player's Untimely Death," *The Sporting Life*, December 19, 1888, 4.

[49] "Notes and Comments," *The Sporting Life*, August 25, 1886, 5.

[50] Ren Mulford, Jr., "Cincinnati Chips," *The Sporting Life*, July 18, 1888, 7.

[51] No title, *The Sporting Life*, February 22, 1888, 2.

[52] "Notes and Comments," *The Sporting Life*, September 12, 1888, 2.

[53] "In Deep Disgrace," *The Sporting Life*, November 14, 1888, 1.

[54] "Glenn's Record," *The Sporting Life*, November 28, 1888, 6.

[55] F. W. Arnold, "Columbus Chatter," *The Sporting Life*, April 3, 1889, 3.

Epilogue

Without doubt, player behaviors such as alcohol abuse, physical fitness, dishonest play, and violence on the field rank among baseball's significant issues in the 1880s. Alcoholism hurt player performance on the field but also hurt the team's potential performance at the ticket office. Having fit and athletic players was important for the same reason. Not only did they increase a team's chance of winning, but most baseball observers also felt they increased a team's profits by providing spectators with quality entertainment that also met the spectators' moral approval. The same also went for on-field violence. Violence disrupted the games, of course, but if the fans started believing that the teams they paid to watch were simply ruffianly brawlers, that was still another reason they might stay away from the ballpark.

This produced an interesting dichotomy when it came to how players behaved and why team management always concerned itself with how their players behaved. In some ways, the interests of the players and their teams were the same. Healthy, sober players who stayed away from brawling and roughhousing tended to be more effective players on the field and tended to live more stable, predictable, and productive lives off the field as well. If they stayed out of trouble and out of the newspapers, team owners could avoid the associated scandal that might tar the image of their teams, or even baseball as an industry.

This last point is where the interests of the two groups diverged. True, most ballplayers probably hoped that the sport they played had a positive image with the public. This image did not directly threaten their livelihood, however, in the way that it did for team ownership. On the one hand, players tended to think as individuals. If they played well, how much money was that worth for the following season? Issues like the game's overall reputation were real but nebulous and hard to translate into a quantifiable number of dollars. Teams, on the other hand, had to think in the aggregate. How might a series of individual decisions impact the team's standing with the public, and how might that increase or decrease overall fan support and ticket revenue? Plus, they also had to decide if a star performer was worth keeping and if the money he produced from excellent play outstripped the amount he might cost the club through undesirable behaviors. Where was the line at which one consideration became more beneficial or costly than the other?

This second set of questions was the reason why teams tried so hard to monitor player drinking and why they encouraged their men to stay in shape year-round. The optimal result was to locate players with good talent and good habits, but if a team could not have both at first, they usually kept trying in the hope of finding the magic formula, rather than part with a talented player. Along the way, they had to swallow hard and hope that players did not start too many brawls, take out their frustrations on obnoxious fans, or injure themselves fighting teammates and the opposition.

Complex as these considerations were, they were only one set of issues influencing the game in the 1880s. This book focuses on things that players did and how teams tried to control those behaviors as best they could. Other issues, however, did not directly involve player behavior but nonetheless exerted great influence over the game and public perceptions of baseball. Those issues are the

Epilogue

focus of another book in this series, *Outside the Lines of Gilded Age Baseball: Gambling, Umpires, and Racism in 1880s Baseball.*

Thank you for reading *Outside the Lines of Gilded Age Baseball: Alcohol, Fitness, and Cheating in 1880s Baseball*. If you enjoyed this book, you can find other books in this series, as well as my works of historical fiction, at my website:

robbauerbooks.com

You can also sign up for my mailing list to receive notifications about future books and promotions. If you enjoyed reading the book, I would be grateful if you'd leave a short review on whatever website you purchased it from. Favorable reader reviews are very important to authors like me. They help tremendously in attracting new readers and spreading the word about existing books you think others will enjoy. Finally, if you like the book, please consider recommending it to fellow baseball fans so they, too, can learn more about the early years of this exciting sport.

Thank you!

Notes on Statistics

It seems that most baseball fans fall into two classes. One consists of those who enjoy watching the game for the excitement and to enjoy the skill of those who play it. They know the rules and the basic strategies of the game, but what concerns them most is the score at the end of the day. If their favorite team wins 90 or more games in a season, they know they have a good team. Their team will probably end up in the playoffs, which means these fans can enjoy watching their heroes for at least another week, maybe longer, and if things break just right, they can celebrate a World Series title when everything is over.

Then there is the second group, whom I refer to as, for lack of a better term and without meaning to sound pejorative at all, the stat heads. These are the folks who intend to analyze everything about baseball, breaking down every event to its mathematical probabilities and contribution to victory or defeat. These are the people who long ago moved beyond the traditional baseball statistics such as wins, earned run average, batting average, runs batted in, and stolen bases. In place of these traditional measures of skill, the stat heads now swear by new metrics such as wins above replacement (WAR), weighted on base average (wOBA), fielding independent pitching (FIP), or batting average on balls in play (BABIP). They have done so for good reason, too. The traditional stats could be quite misleading in terms of how much they indicated regarding a player's contribution to victory. In real world terms, this means that teams often spend lots of money—millions or tens of millions of dollars—on players who do not help them win that many games. Teams focused on traditional statistics, the stat heads point out, embrace a model that is an inefficient way to win baseball games.

The problem is, of course, that books about baseball that one group finds palatable are not as interesting to the other. Fans who appreciate both equally are hard to find. One reason is that it takes effort and a moderate level of mathematical literacy to understand how some statistics work and what they indicate. Calculating batting average is easy, and the statistic has been around forever, so most observers know what numbers equate to a "good" batting average. Divide the number of hits by the number of at bats, and you have batting average. A .300 average is good, a .200 average is poor, and something between .250 and .275 is average. Figuring BABIP is tougher, and it is also new, so most observers are not sure what a "good" BABIP number looks like, much less how to figure out what someone's BABIP is.

The problem goes the other way as well. Some writers and television commentators never tire of pointing out what a "clutch" hitter some player is, for instance. This drives the stat heads nuts because they know that the "ability" to hit in the clutch is not really an ability at all. Given enough at bats to create a proper sample size, a player's performance in tight situations will be close enough to his performance in all situations that there is almost no difference. Some of the stats heads have dedicated themselves to replacing meaningless or misleading statistics with more meaningful ones, and they do not appreciate it when people perpetuate statistical ignorance.

An admission: I really like statistical analysis, and I think it has done a great deal to advance our collective understanding of baseball. In a perfect (baseball) world, I would like to see all fans take the time to become more statistically literate because it opens new ways of seeing the game and understanding what happens on the field and why it matters.

That being said, there is almost no statistical analysis in this book. The main reason is that the book is not about events on the field; rather, it is about the big issues influencing the game and the habits of various players in the 1880s. Furthermore, the people making decisions about how to run teams and win games in the 1880s had no knowledge of the newer statistics some of us depend on today. It would be unfair to criticize them for not using metrics that did not exist. Therefore, the only times I have used statistics is when I want to give the reader a sense of a player's overall quality as part of a brief biographical sketch, and even then, I have tried to use the same ones for consistency. The only nontraditional statistics requiring elaboration the reader will find in this book are:

Wins Above Replacement, or WAR. This is a number that describes how many wins a player was worth beyond what a replacement player would have produced. Statisticians use the concept of a replacement player, rather than an average player, because a replacement player is a borderline major league player or journeyman veteran who is available at low cost. Teams can find them easily without expending many resources to acquire their services. An average player, in contrast, would require resources to acquire and is not freely available, so a team would have to lose something of value, money or another player, to acquire an average player. WAR can be either positive or negative, with a negative WAR indicating the player performed worse than a replacement player would have and cost his team victories with poor play. A player with a single-season WAR between 2.0 and 3.0 is a quality major league player, a WAR around 5.0 is an all-star level player, and someone with a WAR of 7.0 or more is a Most Valuable Player or Cy Young Award candidate most seasons. A team of only replacement players would win about 30% of the time. Another useful thing about WAR is that it works to compare players from vastly different eras. A player with 3.5 WAR in 1888 contributed the same amount to victory as someone with 3.5 WAR in 1988, even if they made their contributions in different ways.

On-Base Percentage Plus Slugging Percentage Plus, or OPS+. I use this measure because research demonstrates that on-base percentage and slugging percentage are the two statistics most correlated with scoring runs, with on-base percentage the most important of the two. Putting the two together in one statistic, therefore, is a good measure of a player's offensive contribution to victory. Some other stats are slightly better measures, perhaps, but in this book I want to give readers a general picture of a player's offensive ability, not a precise analysis, so it will do. The plus means that the number reflects how the player compared to the league average for that season. A player with an OPS+ of 100 was exactly average. Numbers above 100 mean the player exceeded the league average, while an OPS+ below 100 means the player hit worse than an average player that year. Every point above or below 100 equals one percent, so a player with an OPS+ of 110 was ten percent better than average, while someone with a score of 90 was ten percent below average. Once again, this has the added benefit of allowing us to compare the contributions of players across eras.

Earned Run Average Plus, or ERA+. This works just like OPS+, except it describes the earned run average of a pitcher compared to what an average pitcher did that season, so the reader will have a general picture of a pitcher's performance for a given season.

I've also used a batter's "slash" numbers in some cases. These are three numbers, separated by slashes, thus the name. The first number is batting average, the second is on-base percentage, and the third is slugging percentage. Like OPS+, I use this to give the reader a feel for the all-around hitting abilities of the player in question.

That's it. If you understand these few concepts, you know what you need to know to understand the statistics used in this book.

Terminology of the 1880s

All sports have their own terms and ways of referring to the action, and these terms often differ from the regular usage of the word. These words might also have changed meanings since their use on the baseball fields of the 1880s. Here is a short glossary of words used in this book that fit this description.

Battery – The pitcher and catcher.

Box – In the 1880s, the pitcher delivered the ball from the pitcher's box, rather than standing on the pitcher's mound as they do today. We still have the phrase "knocked out of the box," which refers to hitting a pitcher so hard that his team decides to remove the pitcher from the game, even though the pitcher's box itself is no more.

Bulldoze – To argue angrily with, or otherwise try to intimidate, an umpire. Bulldozing was different from kicking, in that bulldozers did not just whine but often threatened the umpire with his position. In the 1880s, the different leagues sometimes removed their umpires if powerful owners complained about the umpire's work too vigorously.

Championship Season – Games in the championship season were what people today call regular season games. Observers called them championship season games because whoever won the most won the league championship and to differentiate them from the frequent exhibition games teams engaged in before, during, and after the championship season.

Coaching – When a player engaged in heckling, trash talking, or similar behaviors. Unlike today, coaching generally did not mean trying to improve a player's performance through instruction.

Condition – A general term describing a player's current state of physical well-being.

Crank – A fan or spectator.

Grounds – The playing field.

Hippodroming – Dishonest playing, usually involving one team throwing a game to another to reward gamblers.

Jonah – A player or team that seemed to be bad luck for another player or team.

Kicking – To argue or complain, especially about the umpire's decisions.

Nine – Used as a synonym for a team. Partly because there were nine players on the field at once and partly because some spectators of the 1880s still remembered when teams had nine total players.

Phenomenal – Like it does today, the word signified a player believed to have exceptional talent. However, observers frequently applied it to up-and-coming young players surrounded by a great deal of hype. Writers sometimes changed the word from an adjective to a noun and used it as a blanket term for such men, writing that their team had signed a phenomenal. Baseball writers referred to one pitcher, John Smith, as a phenomenal so often that Phenomenal Smith became his name while he played ball.

Support – On the field, this meant that a team played quality defense to back up its pitcher. If a team played poor defense, people would write that the team did not support its pitcher.

Work – A reference to the quality of a player's performance. For example, writers described a poor or uninspired performance by writing that a player had done indifferent work.

Bibliography

Books

Alexander, Charles. *Turbulent Seasons: Baseball in 1890-1891*. Dallas: SMU University Press, 2011.

Axelson, Gustav. *COMMY: The Life Story of Charles A. Comiskey*. Chicago: Reilly and Lee Company, 1919.

Cayleff, Susan. *Nature's Path: A History of Naturopathic Healing in America*. Baltimore: Johns Hopkins Press, 2016.

James, Bill. *The New Bill James Historical Baseball Abstract: The Classic—Completely Revised*. New York: The Free Press, 2001.

Leuf, Alexander. *Hygiene for Base Ball Players: Being a Brief Consideration of the Body as a Mechanism; the Art and Science of Curve Pitching; a Discussion of the Causes and Treatment of the Disabilities of Players; With a Few Practical Hints to Club Managers*. Philadelphia: A.J. Reach and Company, 1888.

Mann, Charles. *1493: Uncovering the New World Columbus Created*. New York: Alfred A. Knopf, 2011.

Nemec, David. *The Beer and Whiskey League: The Illustrated History of the American Association—Baseball's Renegade Major League*. New York: Lyons & Burford, 1994.

Pearson, Daniel. *Baseball in 1889: Players vs. Owners*. Bowling Green, OH: Bowling Green State University Popular Press, 1993.

Spalding's Official Base Ball Guide, 1889. Chicago and New York: A.G. Spalding and Bros., 1889.

Stevens, David. *Baseball's Radical for All Seasons: A Biography of John Montgomery Ward.* Lanham, MD: Scarecrow Press, 1998.

Newspapers

Chicago Daily Tribune, 1886-1889

Milwaukee Sentinel, 1887

New York Times, 1885-1888

The Sporting News, 1886-1889

The Sporting Life, 1883, 1885-1889

Websites

Retrosheet, retrosheet.org

Index

A

American Association, 8, 9, 13, 16, 24, 27-29, 31, 34, 43, 44, 53-55, 58, 63, 78-80, 102, 104, 105, 107, 120, 133, 137-139, 150
Anson, Adrian "Cap", 1, 46, 48-50, 67, 75-77, 88, 92, 99, 101, 102, 105, 120, 123, 148
Atlanta, 147, 148
Austria, 76

B

Bakley, Edward, 106
Baldwin, Clarence "Kid", 29, 57, 58, 95, 96, 127, 136
Baltimore, 10, 11, 27, 46, 51-55, 62, 79, 110, 118, 134, 138, 144, 147
Baltimore Orioles, 79, 118, 134, 144, 148
Barkley, Sam, 94, 142
Barnie, Billy, 10, 11, 46, 52-54, 134, 138
Barr, Bob, 122
Bastian, Charlie, 28
Bauer, Al, 138-140
Beatin, Ed, 149
Bell, Bob, 95
Bennett, Charlie, 77, 78, 107, 140
Bierbauer, Lou, 28
Birmingham, Alabama, 100
Bishop, Bill, 94
Boston, 4, 14-16, 26, 47, 59-61, 75, 94, 97, 99, 102, 119, 123, 140, 146
Boston Beaneaters, 16, 59-61, 75, 97, 102, 123, 140
Brennan, Umpire, 55
Brennen, Jack, 153
Briody, Charles "Fatty", 57, 59
Brooklyn, 33, 34, 60, 61, 80, 81, 83, 93, 95, 99, 105, 107, 126, 127, 144

Brooklyn Atlantics, 60
Brooklyn Bridegrooms, 61, 144
Brooklyn Grays, 44, 80
Brotherhood of Professional Baseball Players, 61, 132, 133
Broughton, Cal, 107
Brouthers, Dan, 1, 77, 78, 80, 142
Brown, Lew, 31
Browning, Pete, 16-24, 30, 59, 97, 98
Brunell, Frank, 132, 133, 142
Buckenberger, Al, 111
Buffalo, New York, 100
Buffinton, Charlie, 102
Burch, Ernie, 81
Burdock, Jack, 59-61, 75, 102
Burns, Tom, 46, 91
Burns, Tom "Oyster", 134, 137
Bushong, Doc, 107
Byrne, Charles, 61, 95, 127, 137

C

Cahill, John, 56
Carpenter, Warren "Hick", 127
Carroll, Fred, 146
Cascara sagrada, 104
Casey, Phil, 99
Caylor, Oliver Perry, 8, 10, 108-110, 141
Chadwick, Henry, 46, 56, 67, 109, 110
Chamberlain, Elton, 106
Charleston, South Carolina, 12, 98, 100, 148
Chicago, 1, 14, 31, 42, 46, 49-51, 67, 74, 75, 82, 91, 94, 99, 101, 105, 119, 120, 122, 123, 125, 137, 144, 145, 148, 149
Chicago White Sox, 1
Chicago White Stockings, 42, 47-50, 68, 75, 77, 91-93, 100-102, 105, 121-123, 125, 137, 144, 149
Chimes of Normandy, 145
China, 82
Cinchona tree, 103

Cincinnati, 8-10, 13, 14, 20, 22, 29, 54, 55, 57, 58, 61, 94, 96, 110, 125-127, 136, 139, 142
Cincinnati Reds, 61
Clarkson, John, 1, 75, 82, 122, 140
Cleveland, 20, 33, 54, 79, 95, 99, 106, 132, 140, 142, 146, 147
Cleveland Blues, 33, 79, 95, 106
Cline, Monk, 125
Coaching, 42, 98, 120, 144, 145
Columbus, Ohio, 13, 14, 65, 110, 111, 139, 150
Comiskey, Charlie, 119, 120, 125, 139, 148
Confucius, 82
Connelly, John, 126
Connor, Roger, 1, 5, 33
Constableville, New York, 33
Conway, Pete, 78, 107
Corcoran, Larry, 63
Corkhill, Pop, 127
Crane, Sam, 12
Cuba, 11, 91, 93
Cummins, Andy, 62
Czech Republic, 76

D

Daily, Con, 59, 146
Dalrymple, Abner, 91
Dauvray, Helen, 15
Davidson, Mordecai, 23, 24
Davis, James "Jumbo", 79, 80
Deasley, Tom, 26, 27, 107, 123
Decatur, Alabama, 100
Denny, Jerry, 15, 55, 56, 125, 146
Des Moines, Iowa, 64, 143
Detroit, 48, 57, 65, 77, 100, 107, 119, 148, 149
Detroit Wolverines, 65, 77, 100, 107, 149
Dickerson, Lew, 62-64
Donahue, Jim, 107
Donnelly, Jim, 45

Dorgan, Jerry, 44
Dorgan, Mike, 123

E

Earle, Billy, 14
Esterbrook, Dude, 81
Ewing, Buck, 15, 96, 122

F

Faatz, Jay, 146
Farrell, Jack, 28, 44-46, 53, 54
Fennelly, Frank, 127
Ferguson, Bob, 137, 140
Flint, Silver, 46, 49, 50, 91
Flowers, Dickie, 149
Fogarty, Jim, 123
Foo, Tsang Wong, 82, 83
Force, Davy, 81, 82
Foster, Tom, 137, 138
Foutz, Dave, 81
Foxx, Jimmie, 4
Franz Ferdinand, Archduke, 77
Fraser, Chick, 135
French Lick Springs, Indiana, 18, 22
Fulmer, Chick, 25

G

Gaffney, John, 118
Galvanism, 84
Galvin, Pud, 94
Gardner, Gid, 26, 27
Gifford, Jim, 137
Gilks, Bob, 142
Gilligan, Barney, 45
Gilmore, Frank, 26, 96, 97

Gleason, Bill, 96, 120, 135
Gleason, Jack, 125
Glenn, John, 149, 150
Goldsmith, Fred, 105, 114
Gore, George, 49, 92
Greenwood, Bill, 54, 134

H

Hamilton, Fort, 34
Handball, 90, 94, 96, 99
Hanlon, Ned, 77, 78
Harbridge, Bill, 64
Hecker, Guy, 17, 106
Henderson, Hardie, 104
Hengle, Edward, 125
Henke, Louis, 146
Hillerich and Bradsby, 17
Hines, Paul, 26
Holbert, Bill, 107
Hoover, Buster, 25, 107
Hoover, Charlie, 140
Hornung, Joe, 146
Hot Springs, Arkansas, 12, 74, 75, 77, 91-93, 100-102, 105
Houck, Sadie, 28, 52
Hudson, Nat, 24
Hydropathy, 77

I

Indianapolis, 18, 27, 44, 123, 125, 127, 128, 146
Indianapolis Hoosiers, 44, 125, 128, 146
Indian war clubs, 85, 96
International League, 9, 63, 122

J

James, Bill, 132

Johnston, Dick, 59

K

Kansas City Cowboys, 30, 52, 107, 140
Keefe, Tim, 15, 123
Kelly, John, 19-21, 106
Kelly, Manager, 143
Kelly, Mike, 14-16, 49, 59, 67, 92, 117, 119, 123, 124, 140, 145, 146
Kerins, John, 101, 106, 139
Kilroy, Matt, 118
Kinslow, Tom, 63
Kneipp, Sebastian, 77
Kuehne, Bill, 94

L

LaCrosse, Wisconsin, 100
Larkin, Catherine, 33
Larkin, Frank, 33, 34, 40
Larkin, Henry, 28
Latham, Arlie, 120, 122, 123, 144, 145
Leuf, Alexander, 83-85
Lewis, "Strangler", 95
Lewis, Fred, 8-10, 13, 14, 95
London, Ontario, 63, 64
Louisville, 13, 16-25, 29, 30, 35, 44, 47, 59, 74, 80, 96, 100, 101, 105, 106, 125, 139
Louisville Colonels, 20-23, 35, 44
Lowville, New York, 40
Lucas, Henry, 32
Lynn, Massachusetts, 52
Lyons, Denny, 28

M

Mack, Connie, 26

Macon, Georgia, 100
Madden, Kid, 59
Magnetic healing, 106
Malaria, 102, 103, 108, 109
Manning, Jim, 77, 78
Mantle, Mickey, 4
Marr, Lefty, 65
Marsh, Detroit President, 141
Mason-Dixon Line, 12, 103
Mastoiditis, 18
McAnany, James, 34
McCarthy, Tommy, 136, 138, 140
McClellan, Bill, 61
McCormick, Jim, 46, 49, 59, 92
McGunnigle, Bill, 61
McKim, Kansas City owner, 30
McLaughlin, Tom, 28
McMasters, Jack, 95
McQuaid, John, 127, 140
McTammany, Jim, 143, 144
Memphis, Tennessee, 11, 100, 125
Middletown, Connecticut, 99
Middletown Mansfields, 99
Miller, George, 94
Milwaukee, 11, 21, 100
Minneapolis, 100
Mobile, Alabama, 100, 143
Morrill, John, 15, 16, 97, 102
Morris, Ed, 98, 105
Morrow, Southern League President, 11
Mosquitoes, 103
Mott, Albert, 53, 54, 62
Moxa treatment, 105
Mt. Carmel, Pennsylvania, 11
Mullane, Tony, 142
Murnane, Tim, 99
Murphy, Francis, 21
Murphy, Mike, 83
Mutrie, Jim, 56, 121, 123, 128

N

Nash, Billy, 59, 75, 102
Nashville, 11, 100, 147
National Agreement, 8
National League, 2, 3, 14, 25, 32, 42, 44, 47, 52, 53, 55, 58, 59, 66, 79, 82, 104, 117, 122, 132, 148, 149
National League Constitution, 58
New Orleans, 14, 15, 100
New York, 5, 10, 14, 15, 27, 31, 33, 35-37, 39, 40, 45, 48, 52, 55, 58, 60, 67, 70, 76, 77, 80, 81, 88, 99, 107, 110, 114, 118, 119, 121, 123, 126, 128, 130, 131, 135, 137, 138, 151-153
New York Giants, 14, 15, 33, 55, 56, 81, 118, 121-123, 128
New York Metropolitans, 13, 27, 39, 52, 107, 126, 135, 137
Nichols, Thomas, 76
Nicol, Hugh, 95, 96, 118, 119, 123, 125

O

Oriole Park, 54
O'Brien, Darby, 144
O'Brien, Jack, 135
O'Connor, Jack, 61, 62, 110
O'Neill, Tip, 135
O'Rourke, Jim, 118, 121
O'Rourke, Tom, 59

P

Palmer, Harry, 75, 91-93
Palmyra, New York, 99
Patterson, William, 106
Pfeffer, Fred, 125
Phelps, Zach, 18, 47, 138
Philadelphia, 4, 15, 27-29, 35, 45, 63, 65, 96, 98, 102, 103, 110, 123, 129, 133, 149

Philadelphia Athletics, 13, 27-30, 35, 45, 52, 102, 110, 129, 133, 149
Philadelphia Phillies, 63, 98
Philadelphia Quakers, 15, 45, 65, 98, 123
Phillips, Bill, 93
Phillips, Horace, 48, 100, 110, 128, 148
Phillips, Marr, 148
Pierson, Dave, 137
Pinkerton Detective Agency, 46, 48, 49
Pittsburgh, 47, 48, 50, 59, 94, 95, 100, 105, 110, 127, 128, 145, 148
Plasmodium vivex, 103
Polo Grounds, New York, 123, 128
Poorman, Tom, 75
Porter, Henry, 126
Portland, Maine, 62, 63
Potassium bromide, 64
Powell, Abner, 25
Priessnitz, Vincent, 76
Pritchard, Joe, 133
Prostitution, 108
Providence, Rhode Island, 28, 32, 44, 45

Q

Quest, Joe, 117

R

Radbourn, Charlie, 59, 97, 98
Ramsey, Tom, 16-24, 30, 106
Reach, Al, 85
Reach Exercise Machine, 85
Reilly, John, 78, 127, 136
Reynolds, Charlie, 107
Richardson, Danny, 56, 78
Richardson, Hardy, 77, 78
Richmond Virginians, 34

Ridgewood Park, Brooklyn, 144
Ringo, Frank, 30, 31
Robinson, Yank, 133, 135, 139, 144
Rochester, New York, 9, 10, 106
Rockford, Illinois, 95
Roosevelt, Theodore, 77
Roseman, Chief, 27

S

Sacramento, California, 33
Sacramento Altas, 33, 65
Savannah, Georgia, 64, 100
Scandrett, A. K., 50
Scanlon, Mike, 25, 121
Schmelz, Gus, 51, 58, 97, 139
Schomberg, Otto, 146
Scranton, Pennsylvania, 12
Seery, Emmett, 32, 145
Seneca Falls, New York, 99
Sharsig, Billy, 29, 45
Shew, Joel, 76
Shindle, Billy, 144
Shoeneck, Jumbo, 147
Simmons, Newark infielder, 147
Slattery, Mike, 81
Smith, Charles, 94
Smith, George, 95
Smith, Phenomenal, 79, 137
Sommers, Andy, 107
Spalding, Al, 42, 46-50, 59, 66, 74, 77, 82, 93, 101, 102, 109
Sportsman's Park, St. Louis, 55, 94, 118, 135, 138
St. Louis, 8, 11, 17, 18, 20, 24, 27-29, 31, 32, 49-51, 54-56, 58, 61,
    94, 96, 105, 118-120, 123, 124, 129, 133, 135, 136, 138, 139,
    144, 147, 148
St. Louis Browns, 8, 18, 24, 27-29, 49, 58, 61, 94, 118, 120, 121,
    123-125, 129, 133-136, 144, 148
St. Louis Maroons, 51, 55, 138

St. Mary's hospital, Brooklyn, 83
Stackhouse, George, 80, 81
Staten Island, New York, 135
Stemmyer, Bill, 59, 75
Stovey, Harry, 28, 98
Sullivan, John L., 17
Sullivan, Ted, 135, 139
Sulphur Springs, Arkansas, 75
Sutcliffe, Sy, 122
Sutton, Ezra, 99, 102
Swampdoodle Grounds, Washington, D. C., 27
Swarthmore College, Pennsylvania, 83
Swartwood, Ed, 104
Sweeney, Charlie, 32, 33, 64
Sweeney, Rooney, 107
Syracuse, New York, 33, 64, 100
Syracuse Stars, 33, 100

T

Taylor, Billy, 8, 10-14, 64, 104, 117, 123
Terry, Adonis, 99
Thompson, Sam, 77, 78, 80
Toledo, Ohio, 134
Toronto, 100
Trexlertown, Pennsylvania, 149
Tri-State League, 139
Triumvirs (Boston owners), 47, 59
Troy Haymakers, 149
Tucker, Tommy, 118
Twitchell, Larry, 77, 78

U

Union Association, 32
University of Pennsylvania, 83
Utica, New York, 10, 100

V

Veach, "Peek-A-Boo", 64-66
Viau, Lee, 126, 127
Von der Ahe, Chris, 8, 9, 29, 30, 55, 94, 138
Vonderhorst, Harry, 54

W

Wagner, Honus, 3
Ward, John Montgomery, 1, 5, 15, 55, 61, 119
Washington, D. C., 26, 27, 45, 47, 121, 137
Washington Nationals, 25, 27, 45, 95, 96, 121
Washington Park, Brooklyn, 60
Welch, Curt, 5, 28, 94, 133-135, 148
Weyhing, Gus, 133-135
Weyhing, John, 111
Whalen, Peter, 149
Wheelock, Bobby, 59
White, Bill, 25
White, Deacon, 78
Widner, Bill, 110, 111
Williams, Jimmy, 112
Williamson, Ned, 46, 49, 75, 76, 91-93, 125
Wise, Sam, 59, 75, 102, 146
Wood, George, 65, 66
Wood, Pete, 122
Wright, Harry, 15, 45, 62, 94, 98, 103

Y

Young Men's Christian Association (YMCA), 98

ABOUT THE AUTHOR

I'm Rob Bauer, author of historical fiction and nonfiction books and owner of Rob Bauer Books. I hold a PhD in American History and was a Distinguished Doctoral Fellow at the University of Arkansas.

My fiction has two purposes—entertaining readers and explaining historical injustice. Although I enjoy adventure and humorous books as much as the next reader, I'd like my books to stand for something a little bigger. All my studies in history put me in a position to do that. Whether I'm writing about how racism damages the individual psyche, the deportation of the Métis people of Montana, the South's prison labor system, or the utter terror of the Belgian Congo, with my books you'll find yourself in powerful historical stories.

I also write nonfiction about baseball history because I've always loved the game, its history, and its lore. I sometimes joke that baseball may be the one thing in life I truly understand. Although I love the statistical side of the game, if you don't, never fear because my histories go light on the statistics and heavy on what baseball was like in the past. They're stories about baseball, but stories with a point.

The history blog on my website offers posts on a variety of interesting historical figures and events. I'd love to have you follow along.

When I'm not working on my next story or writing project, I enjoy spending time at the beach. And, oh yeah, I still read a history book or two. When I'm not watching baseball.

ACKNOWLEDGMENTS

I also want to thank the people who helped make this book possible, especially Jim Soular for his help with editing. Ali Holst gets the credit for the cover art and design. Thank you to David Mitchell for his commentary on sample chapters. Finally, thank you to Elliott West, my peerless dissertation advisor at the University of Arkansas, for having the courage to approve this as a dissertation topic and allow me to start this research in the first place.

Made in the USA
Middletown, DE
23 December 2020